THE NUCLEAR ENERGY CONTROVERSY

THE NUCLEAR ENERGY CONTROVERSY

BY STEPHEN GOODE

333.79
Goo

8722

Blairsville Junior High School
Blairsville, Pennsylvania

Franklin Watts
New York | London | Sydney | Toronto | 1980
An Impact Book

Photographs courtesy of: Argonne National Laboratory: pp. 30–31; United Press International: pp. 34, 78–79; Westinghouse Photo by Jack Merhaut: p. 60; Iowa Electric Light & Power Co.: p. 37.

Illustrations courtesy of Vantage Art, Inc.

Library of Congress Cataloging in Publication Data

Goode, Stephen.
The nuclear energy controversy.

(An Impact book)
Bibliography: p.
Includes index.
SUMMARY: Discusses the positive and negative aspects of nuclear energy and the controversy surrounding the use of this type of energy.
1. Atomic power—Juvenile literature. 2. Atomic power-plants—Juvenile literature. [1. Atomic power. 2. Atomic power plants] I. Title.
TK9148.G66   333.79′24   80–14484
ISBN 0–531–04165–4

CONTENTS

THE NUCLEAR ENERGY CONTROVERSY

CHAPTER 1
THE PROBLEM

The world is in the midst of an energy crisis. The nature of the crisis can be stated simply, but its possible solutions are overwhelming in their complexity. There is not enough energy available at present to supply everyone's hopes and needs. The industrial nations—the United States, Canada, Japan, and the countries of Western and Eastern Europe—need ever-increasing supplies of fuel to maintain their standards of living and to keep people at work. At the same time, the underdeveloped regions of the world—the nations of Africa, Asia, and South America—hope to end age-old cycles of poverty and economic lethargy by the establishment of modern technology. They too want to share in the energy-devouring advantages of progress and modernization.

Where is all this energy supposed to come from? Oil—the chief source of energy for the industrialized nations—is growing scarce and more expensive. In an article in *Scientific American,* (March, 1978), Andrew Flower, a policy analyst with the British Petroleum Company, estimates that by the year 2000, the decreasing supply of oil will fail to meet the world's increasing demands for it. By that time, he warns, there will be too little oil to run machines and automobiles, supply electricity, or provide the energy needs of the world. The price of oil will become prohibitive, placing severe economic strain on the wealthy nations, while making industrial development among the poor countries an impossibility.

The outlook for other forms of energy is also uncertain. Natural gas, like oil, is a "nonrenewable resource" that will someday—probably within the next thirty to forty years—become scarce and eventually run out. The world's supply of coal is still large and could provide a source of power for many years to come. But the use of coal creates severe pollution and environmental problems. The burning of coal yields a number of chemicals that contaminate the atmosphere, while coal mines leak acids into nearby streams. Technology has provided a number of methods to reduce pollution, but these methods remain expensive and help to drive up the cost of the use of coal. Once again, we are faced with a source of energy that will become increasingly costly as time passes.

The production of synthetic fuels from coal and oil shale, hydroelectric energy, geothermal energy, solar energy, and the harnessing of the power of the wind have also been offered as solutions to the energy crisis. But these programs too have their disagreeable and troublesome aspects. Synthetic fuels—which form an important part of President Jimmy Carter's energy plans for the United States—are expensive to produce and, in addition, pollute the atmosphere with a variety of chemicals including cancer-causing polycyclic hydrocarbons.

Solar energy, which will provide power for the world from the rays of the sun, seems to be the hope of the distant future. At the present time, its development is slowed down due to doubts about the effectiveness of solar technology and fears concerning its costs. Many experts believe it will be fifty years before we shall know how to harness efficiently the rays of the sun and turn the sun's power to our own uses; others believe that solar technology can develop much sooner. However, most agree that hydroelectric power and geothermal energy (tapping the heat inside the earth and using it to produce energy) are either incapable of supplying all the energy the world needs or too difficult to develop at this time.

One other source of energy that is frequently mentioned is nuclear energy, the power that is released when the nucleus, or core, of a complex atom divides to form simpler atoms.* Nuclear energy now generates about 13 percent of the electricity produced in the United States and there are plans to increase that percentage rapidly to meet the growing scarcity of oil. For many scientists and energy experts, nuclear energy is the answer that happened at the right moment to save us all from the disaster of the energy crisis. The power of the atom, they believe, can supply the world with enormous amounts of energy for years to come.

But for many others, nuclear energy offers no solution to our energy problems at all. For these people—and their number includes scientists, environmentalists, and gifted and determined men and women from a variety of fields— nuclear energy is a nightmare that must be brought to an end. They fear that the expansion of the nuclear industry will lead to radioactive contamination of the planet and widespread death and sickness due to radioactive poisoning, cancer, and birth defects. The present energy crisis, they warn, should not blind us to the dangers of nuclear power.

ATOMS FOR PEACE
In recent years, the nuclear energy controversy has aroused more disagreement, public concern, and even anger than controversies surrounding any other source of power. But this has not always been so. When President Dwight D. Eisenhower launched his Atoms for Peace program in 1953, the general feeling toward nuclear power was optimistic and

---

* The splitting, or dividing, of atoms is known as fission. At present, all nuclear power plants derive their power from fission. But scientists are also experimenting with fusion, which is the joining of smaller nuclei to form more complex nuclei. Fusion also releases a great deal of energy, but as yet the use of fusion to produce electricity commercially is not in the scope of our technology.

hopeful. Until that time, nuclear power had been the province of the military under whose direction the atomic and hydrogen bombs were developed. But now, Eisenhower promised, the same expertise that built the bombs would be used to develop nuclear reactors. These reactors would increase the availability of electricity not only in the United States, but would eventually help to raise the standard of life throughout the world.

The optimism of the time was reflected in *Report on the Atom,* a book published in 1953 by Gordon Dean, a former chairman of the U.S. Atomic Energy Commission (AEC). Dean predicted that the near future would bring nuclear-generated electricity, nuclear-powered submarines and surface craft, and perhaps nuclear airplanes and locomotives. Atomic energy, he concluded, could improve the economic condition of the world in three ways. "It can provide a new, inexpensive source of power that can help reduce industrial production costs in many parts of Europe and elsewhere; it can create new markets for the industrial production of Europe and America by helping to open up and develop the backward areas of the world; and, while it is building, it can create new demands for technical equipment and materials that can inject a fresh life into the industrial economy of the West."

Other publications were even more optimistic. In *Your Friend the Atom,* a readable and useful account of atomic energy for younger readers, Heinz Haber, the chief science consultant of Walt Disney Productions, compared nuclear power to the genie of myth and legend. Like the genie, Haber wrote, nuclear power offers humanity the fulfillment of three great wishes. First, it fulfills the wish for a source of energy that will serve the world for a long time. Next, through the use of radioisotopes, nuclear energy offers a means to study plant life, so that science can increase the production of food. And, finally, nuclear energy grants us a wish that is at the same time a responsibility. By studying the atom, we can join in the work of the world's great scientists—Madame Curie, Einstein, and others—and see that the atom is used for peaceful purposes rather than for war. If these three wishes are answered, Haber wrote, "then the atom will become truly our friend."

The great appeal of nuclear energy was its relative cleanliness and its cheapness. Gordon Dean, the former head of the AEC, argued that nuclear power would make our cities "a cleaner and more attractive place in which to live" because "no smoke or fumes" emerge from a nuclear power plant. At a time when there were few pollution controls placed on the burning of coal or oil, this promise of an atmosphere less soiled by industrial wastes held a strong appeal to many people. If atomic power meant less smog and soot, then it was indeed an attractive source of energy.

The costs of nuclear energy were also attractive and appealing. In the mid-fifties, it was estimated that 9 kilograms (20 pounds) of uranium could provide enough power to light twenty-five thousand average-sized homes in the United States for a whole year. Since the cost of refined uranium in 1955 was about $35 a pound, this meant that twenty-five thousand homes could be lighted at a total cost of $700, or slightly under three cents per year for each household. This was cheaper than the cost of electricity produced by coal or oil, and implied that budget-minded Americans would soon be able to save money on fuel and energy bills.

In 1954, the United States initiated a five-year program designed to produce nuclear reactors that were large enough to generate significant amounts of electricity. The government granted liberal subsidies to private firms and universities to carry out research in the nuclear field. From among more than eighty nuclear reactor types whose designs had been planned or sketched, five were chosen as most worthy of consideration and development. The five-year project—which was known as the experimental-reactor program—would concentrate on these five reactors and iron out any problems involved in their future use.

Work was begun on the first full-scale nuclear power plant for civilian use, with plans for its completion in 1957 (it was in fact completed in 1958). Located in Shippingport, Pennsylvania, not far from the industrial city of Pittsburgh, this reactor was to be a *pressurized-water reactor* (PWR) and was to produce 65,000 kilowatts of electricity. The reactor was similar in design to others already developed by the nuclear program of the American military since World War II.

The Shippingport plant was small compared to many oil- and coal-burning utility plants, but it was hoped that it would be large enough to provide experience and practical knowledge that could be used by nuclear engineers and scientists in the development of larger nuclear plants in the future. In addition, the Joint Congressional Committee on Atomic Energy believed that the plant at Shippingport would serve as proof to the world of America's intention to use atomic power peacefully.

Since the development of the first nuclear plant, the American nuclear industry has developed into a large and important segment of the American economy. There are now seventy-two commercial nuclear reactor plants in the United States, although not all of them are in operation, and there are plans to expand the industry rapidly by the early years of the next century. Eventually, nuclear experts hope to see 150 to 350 large reactors producing the electricity needed for economic progress and expansion. Some have even hoped for as many as 750 to 1,000. These reactors would include a number of "breeder" reactors, so called because they produce more fuel than they use up. Once this network of breeders and conventional reactors has been established, the experts assure us, the energy crisis will be a thing of the past.

Today, however, the period of early optimism and hope for nuclear energy has come to an end. Nuclear energy is in trouble. In 1980, little more than a quarter century after President Eisenhower announced his Atoms for Peace program, large segments of public opinion oppose the use of nuclear reactors and atomic energy. The production of reactors in the United States has come to a near standstill and the nuclear future foreseen by the experts is clouded with uncertainty and bitter disagreement.

Why has nuclear energy come to be regarded by some as a monster that needs to be controlled or destroyed instead of a blessing and panacea that would solve our energy needs? The answer lies in two areas: economics and safety. The early pioneers in reactor research did not disregard these problems. They recognized that many aspects of nuclear energy might prove expensive and would involve hazards to human health and to the environment. But they likewise believed that these problems would be solved in time, as men and women worked on them and found adequate solutions.

The problem of expense, the experts believed, would shrink as more knowledge about reactors and how they worked was accumulated. Once reactors were mass-produced, their prices would come down. This, however, has not been the case. The costs of reactors have climbed enormously in the past twenty years. Furthermore, reactors themselves have proved to be less than foolproof. Many are forced to shut down, often for long periods of time, for repairs or other reasons, leaving them unproductive and forcing utility companies to buy other forms of fuel. Nuclear energy, in most cases, has not been the inexpensive source of energy pictured by its advocates, while critics of nuclear energy complain that nuclear costs will continue to rise and create ever higher bills for consumers.

The problem of safety provides an even more difficult question for nuclear advocates to answer. Science has made great strides in the improvement of reactors, but these improvements have not convinced nuclear critics that nuclear energy is safe and harmless. The critics argue that the use of nuclear energy creates numerous chances for the release of dangerous radioactive materials, from the time uranium is mined and processed until the "spent," or used fuel in the reactor is ready for disposal. The radioactive wastes from reactors, the critics point out, will remain toxic for thousands of years, endangering the lives of future generations.

The antinuclear people are concerned too that a serious

- ● Boiling-Water Reactor
- ■ Pressurized-Water Reactor
- ▲ High Temperature Gas Reactor

Nuclear Power Reactors in the United States

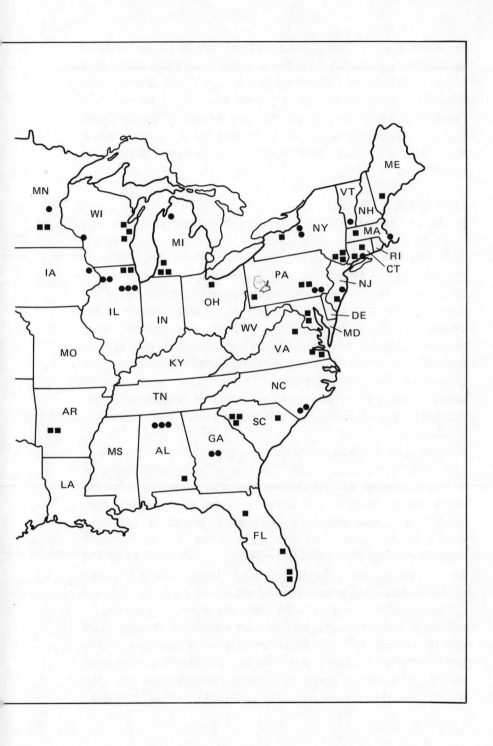

accident at a nuclear plant could release large amounts of radioactivity suddenly into the atmosphere. They worry that a group of terrorists might steal uranium or plutonium from a reactor plant and build a bomb that could be used to threaten a large city or blackmail the American government. If these are the risks we run by opting for a nuclear future, the critics conclude, then our nuclear program should be abandoned.

THREE MILE ISLAND

In the spring of 1979 an incident occurred that strongly dramatized both of the problems involved with nuclear energy—its expensiveness and the question of safety. Early on the morning of March 28, a large reactor at Three Mile Island in central Pennsylvania began to malfunction. Over the next few days, a series of mechanical and human errors created a crisis of major proportions. The governor of Pennsylvania, fearful of the hazards of radioactivity, recommended the evacuation of pregnant women and small children from the immediate area. Thousands of other people also left, while hundreds of newspaper and television reporters from around the world arrived to cover the impending disaster.

Three possibilities bothered the experts and officials in charge at Three Mile Island. The first was radiation leakage. A small amount of radioactive gas had escaped from the plant the morning of the accident. How much would continue to leak, how could the leakage be controlled, and what would be the effects of this leakage on the surrounding neighborhood? The experts hoped to confine most of the dangerous radioactivity to the plant itself, where it could be confined and eventually disposed of.

The other two possibilities were far more frightening. A bubble of hydrogen gas had formed inside the reactor plant and threatened to explode, sending large amounts of highly toxic radioactive substances into the air. Such an explosion would contaminate much of central Pennsylvania and perhaps prove dangerous to major population areas that were not far away—Philadelphia, Baltimore, and Washington, D.C. The question of how to dissolve the bubble before it blew up the reactor, quickly became one of the most important problems the scientists and engineers at Three Mile Island had to solve.

At the same time, the experts realized that the reactor core—which contains the radioactive fuel of the reactor—had become so hot that a "meltdown" was also a possibility. In a meltdown, the uranium in the core becomes so heated that it melts through the floor of the plant and continues to sink into the ground until it has been sufficiently cooled by rock and dirt.* The highly radioactive material is then underground, where it can pollute water supplies and render them unusable for a long period of time.

The disaster at Three Mile Island, however, was contained and brought under control. The hydrogen bubble was dissolved before it exploded. Later investigations showed that even if the bubble had exploded, the explosion would not have been strong enough to destroy the reactor containment or the hard rock underneath. The reactor core did not experience a meltdown. Radioactive leakage from the plant remained small and seemed to pose no significant problem for the people of the surrounding area. But the incident dealt a severe blow to the nuclear energy industry and it will be some time, if ever, before the public will look upon nuclear power without misgivings and uncertainty.

The events at Three Mile Island displayed the expense of nuclear energy in glaring terms. The reactor itself had cost a great deal of money, but had proved faulty from the time it first went into commercial operation on December 31, 1978, only three months before the accident. The costs of cleanup will be enormous and there is some question whether the reactor will ever generate electricity again. Moreover, the utility company that owns the reactor will pass the expenses that have developed since the accident on to

* A meltdown is also known, more colorfully, as the China syndrome, since one can imagine a reactor so hot that it melts its way through the earth, appearing eventually in China.

the consumers in the form of higher electric bills. If this is the price that must be paid for nuclear energy, the average consumer might ask, wouldn't it be wiser to find another source of power?

Three Mile Island also called the safety of reactors into question as never before. Investigations of the accident showed that a series of human and mechanical errors had led to the leakage of radioactive material, the formation of the hydrogen bubble, and the exposure of the reactor core. These errors had been kept under control in this instance, but who could say when another nuclear accident might get out of hand?

In addition, nuclear experts at the reactor site publicly disagreed on what had happened and on what steps needed to be taken to render the reactor harmless. These disagreements increased anxiety and concern, because they aroused fears that no one knew what to do in this emergency. The disagreements and bickering also gave rise to suspicions that some officials were attempting to hide the truth about the accident from the public and make it sound much less dangerous than it actually was.

Finally, Three Mile Island raised the question of the safe disposal of nuclear wastes. Several states have declared that radioactive material from Three Mile Island cannot be transported on their roads or highways, while South Carolina, where the wastes were to be stored, has declined to allow the material to remain within its borders. For some time to come Three Mile Island will remain a headache for the nuclear community.

The nuclear energy controversy has become one of the important issues of our time. At stake are problems that involve the economy, politics, the environment, and the health of every living thing. On one hand, nuclear proponents tell us that nuclear energy is the only relatively safe, inexpensive, and reliable means to solve the energy crisis. On the other hand, the critics warn us that nuclear power is a certain prescription for disaster.

This book will look at the questions involved in the nuclear debate. First, we shall look at the nature of nuclear energy and then at the functioning and structure of nuclear reactors. But the central and largest portion of the book will deal with controversy over nuclear energy itself. The best arguments on both sides will be given in the hope that the reader can resolve his or her own opinion. The issues are bitterly contested, but men and women of wisdom and learning stand on both sides.

CHAPTER 2
THE NATURE OF NUCLEAR ENERGY

The discovery of nuclear energy came as a result of numerous scientific investigations into the nature of matter and how matter is formed. The men and women who conducted these investigations at first had little inkling of the enormous source of power they were about to uncover. As time passed, however, and as experiment after experiment filled in gaps of missing knowledge, it became clear that science had succeeded in interpreting the world as it had never been interpreted before. What had begun as an exercise of scientific curiosity ended in giving the world greater understanding of reality and the ability to harness the basic energy of the universe.

The man who can be regarded as the father of modern atomic theory is John Dalton, a British chemist. In 1808, after years of experimentation and close observation, he theorized that the basic unit of all matter was a tiny particle called the atom, after the Greek word for "something that cannot be cut or divided." He imagined atoms to be like incredibly small balls or marbles and suspected that they were held together by powerful forces in order to form solids such as silver or steel.

Dalton's theory was not entirely new. Ancient Greek philosophers had speculated that the world was made up of innumerable small particles that combined and recombined to form various objects. But Dalton added something the ancient Greeks had not. He believed that the atoms of different basic substances, called elements, had different weights. He argued, for instance, that the atom of oxygen was eight times heavier than the atom of hydrogen. In this, Dalton was wrong—the oxygen atom was later found to be sixteen times heavier than the hydrogen atom—but his mistake amounted to little more than an error in simple arithmetic. Much of Dalton's atomic theory was correct and helped to prepare the way for the startling new discoveries in chemistry and physics that were to come.

In 1811, the Italian physicist Amadeo Avogadro carried Dalton's work one step further. Avogadro discovered that Dalton's atoms combine in regular patterns to form the substances that make up the world. Two atoms of hydrogen unite with one atom of oxygen to form water; similarly, sodium chloride, or common table salt, was always formed by the union of one atom of sodium and one atom of chlorine. Avogadro called these groups of atoms that formed substances molecules, after the Latin word *molecula,* meaning little bundles.

Since the time of Dalton and Avogadro, scientists have discovered the existence of ninety-two elements in nature (several others have been artificially produced in laboratories). Each of these elements, as Dalton theorized, has distinctive characteristics that distinguish it from all other elements. Some elements have familiar names like gold, sulphur, iron, or helium; others have rare and exotic names like ytterbium or vanadium. At the same time, science has explored the nature of molecules, from the most simple— such as water or table salt—to the most complex, which sometimes contain hundreds of thousands of atoms.

For a long time, atoms and the molecules that were made up of atoms appeared to be the basic building units of nature. The way in which atoms and molecules combine or in which they react to changes in temperature and pressure seemed to explain much that had never been understood in chemistry and physics. By the end of the nineteenth century, however, new experiments had uncovered evidence that led many scientists to conclude that the atom itself could be divided into constituent parts. It was not, as many had believed, a tiny marble that could not be broken up. Instead, it was an entity with a structure all its own and was composed of even smaller units that sometimes broke away from the atom and functioned alone.

Some of the first evidence for the existence of particles smaller than atoms came from experimentation in the field of electricity. For many years, scientists had studied the behavior of a "cathode tube," which is a closed column of glass that has a negative electrical plate called a cathode and a positive plate, or anode, attached to it. When pressure is reduced in the tube and the proper amount of electricity is applied, the tube will give off a glow—this is the principle behind the neon sign. But when the pressure in the tube is further reduced, the glow stops and the tube becomes dark. At this time, a strange emission appears at one end of the tube and travels to the other, where small sparks of light are created when the emission strikes the glass at the tube's end.

The nature of this emission puzzled the scientists who investigated it. Was it a series of particles or was it in the form of rays, similar to the rays of the sun? In 1897, the English physicist, J. J. Thomson, found the answer—the emission was a series of particles. Thomson also discovered that the particles were very small and that they were 1,840 times smaller than the hydrogen atom, the smallest known atom. He estimated that the particles, which we now call electrons, traveled at the speed of 29,900 kilometers (18,600 miles) per second or about one-tenth the speed of light.

Further experimentation caused Thomson to conclude that the electrons were parts of the atom. He designed a special apparatus called a discharge tube to prove this theory. When hydrogen gas alone was placed in the tube and an electric current was passed through it, the familiar series of electrons appeared. At the same time, however, there was also a series of positive particles in the discharge tube.

These positive particles were almost the same weight as single hydrogen atoms.

When Thomson repeated the experiment using oxygen instead of hydrogen, he obtained similar results. The series of electrons appeared. But this time, the positive particles were almost the same weight as oxygen atoms, rather than hydrogen atoms. What had happened, apparently, was that the electric current in the discharge tube caused the hydrogen and oxygen atoms to divide into a negative unit— the electron—and a positive unit. It would be several years before the nature of the positive unit was understood, but Thomson had uncovered some of the secrets that would lead to the development of nuclear energy.

Meanwhile, discoveries in other areas of physics were shedding new light on the nature of the atom. In 1895, W. C. Röntgen, a German physicist, discovered that rays emitted from a tube similar to a cathode tube had great penetrating ability. The rays could pierce a layer of cardboard and even go through several inches of wood or thin sheets of aluminum. Röntgen also found that these rays—which he called X rays because he did not understand their origin—would easily pass through human flesh and leave pictures of the inner body on specially coated paper. Soon doctors were using X rays to study human problems and discover broken bones. What puzzled Röntgen and other physicists about X rays, however, was how they were able to pass through matter so easily. Obviously, some new explanation of how materials were put together was necessary to account for how seemingly solid things—like wood or aluminum—could be pierced without effort.

THE DISCOVERY OF RADIOACTIVITY

The discovery of X rays was unexpected and almost accidental. This was also true of the discovery of radioactivity, whose disclosure caused scientists to modify their ideas of atoms even further. In 1896, Henri Becquerel, a Frenchman, was experimenting with a crystal of potassium uranyl sulphate, a compound that contained the element uranium. Becquerel found that the crystal would leave an image of itself on a photographic plate, even when the crystal and the plate were in total darkness. At first, he thought that sunlight activated something within the crystal which gave it the power to emit rays when placed in darkness. But later, he discovered that the crystal would emit the rays even when it had not been exposed to sunlight.

The discovery was extraordinary. Here was a substance that seemed to produce some sort of power on its own, as part of a natural process that went on without stimulation. Soon other scientists became interested in this new phenomenon. In France, Marie Curie, a chemist, and her physicist husband, Pierre, began to work with a large supply of uranium ore. To their surprise, they found that there were other elements, also radioactive, present in their sample.

In addition to the uranium, there was polonium, which they named for Marie's native Poland, and a small amount of what they called radium. The radium was so highly radioactive that it would keep itself noticeably warmer than the air around it. In other words, the radium was producing energy by some unknown means and at such a rate that it was able to heat itself—and to go on heating itself with no seeming loss of power.

What was the nature of radioactivity and where did it come from? Some of the first answers to these questions were supplied by Ernest Rutherford, a New Zealander whose laboratory was located in Cambridge, England. Working with uranium, Rutherford discovered two kinds of radiation. One kind would penetrate the air around the uranium sample only a few inches before its force was dissipated, and a second type could penetrate much farther.

Rutherford called the first type of radiation, the weaker one, alpha particles, after the first letter of the Greek alphabet. The stronger rays he called beta particles, after the second letter. Further investigation showed that alpha particles traveled about 10 centimeters (4 inches) before they were stopped, and that they could be brought to a halt by a small thickness of aluminum. Beta particles, on the other hand, were found to be about one hundred times more penetrating than alpha particles.

In 1900, Paul Villard, a French scientist, found a third type of radiation emitted from radioactive substances. Villard's radiation was called gamma rays, after the third letter of the Greek alphabet, and was discovered to be far stronger than either alpha or beta particles. Indeed, gamma rays could penetrate a piece of iron 30 centimeters (12 inches) thick, but would be stopped by several inches of lead.

Thus far, science had recorded the existence of radioactivity and noted its power, but no one had discovered just what radioactivity was. Here too the work of Ernest Rutherford was important. Rutherford first looked into the nature of alpha particles by using a sample of the recently discovered element radium. He placed a small amount of radium in a container and then placed the container in a larger tube. The air in the larger tube was then pumped out.

Sometime later, Rutherford took a reading of the atmosphere in the tube to see if it now contained anything. It did: helium atoms. Rutherford concluded that the helium had come from the radium and that alpha particles and helium were similar. However, there was one difference that he noted. Alpha particles were similar to helium atoms, but they were helium atoms that had shed electrons and had become positively charged. Rutherford's experiments also showed that alpha particles had a speed of about 13,700 to 20,100 kilometers (8,500 to 12,500 miles) per second.

Beta particles, on the other hand, were found to be negatively charged particles. They were electrons traveling at very high speeds, sometimes approaching the speed of light, or about 300,000 kilometers (186,000 miles) per second. Gamma rays yielded their secrets more slowly. It was not until 1914 that Rutherford found gamma rays, which have no electrical charge, to be similar to X rays, but with an extremely short wavelength.

As a result of their early investigations into the nature of radioactivity, Rutherford and his assistant, F. Soddy, put forth "the disintegration theory of radioactivity" in 1902. Radioactivity, they said, was a process whereby an unstable element, such as uranium, radium, or polonium, shed particles to become a new element. This new element too might be radioactive and continue to shed particles—alpha particles or positively charged helium atoms, beta particles or electrons, and gamma rays—until a stable element, like lead, was formed.

Rutherford and Soddy's theory was not widely accepted at first by the scientific community. It undermined the notion popular since Dalton that atoms were indivisible and the atoms of one element could not be changed into the atoms of another. But the theory stood the test of time. Subsequent experimentation showed it to be correct. Certain unstable elements did change in time and become new elements. And in the process, it was noted, a certain amount of energy was released that often warmed the radioactive material and made it warmer than its surroundings. The nature and degree of that energy, however, were not yet understood.

Science now knew about the existence of the electron and suspected that electrons formed part of an atom. It knew about the "positively charged particles" that J. J. Thomson found in his discharge tube and it knew about radioactivity—the particles and rays emitted by certain elements. But how did all this information fit together? How could the easy penetration of matter by radioactivity be explained and what could account for the existence of particles smaller than atoms?

The answers came in bits and pieces between 1907 and 1913. First, Rutherford, in a brilliant series of experiments, determined that the positively charged particle of an atom was always located in the atom's center. He called this concentrated positive charge the nucleus (plural, nuclei) from the Latin word for "kernel" or "nut." The electrons on negatively charged particles Rutherford placed at a distance from the nucleus and he theorized that they whirled around the nucleus at great speeds, in order to keep from being pulled into the center of the atom, much like the speed of the earth around the sun keeps it from falling into the sun.

How did X rays and alpha and beta particles penetrate matter? They did so by passing through the immense space between the nucleus of the atom and the electrons. Remember that we are dealing with very small particles. It takes billions and billions of atoms to make the head of a match. The nucleus and electrons are even smaller, yet between the nucleus and electrons there is more than enough space to allow radiation to pass through.

In 1913, the brilliant Danish theoretical physicist, Niels Bohr, offered a more sophisticated model of the atom, based on the work of Rutherford. Bohr placed the nucleus at the center of the atom with electrons in orbit. He estimated that one electron whirled around the nucleus seven million billion times every second, a speed so great that a veritable shield or shell was formed. Sometimes an electron changed orbits, from a low-energy orbit to one with higher energy or from a high-energy orbit to one with lower energy. When atoms combined to form molecules, the different atoms shared electrons, thereby forming the linkage that made chemical compounds—like water or sodium chloride—possible.

Bohr's model of the atom has been replaced in nuclear physics by more complex models that can only be expressed with mathematical equations. Yet for our purposes, it is still useful. It is the atomic model familiar to every science student. Using Bohr's suggestions, a hydrogen atom —the simplest atom in nature—can be viewed as a nucleus consisting of a single proton which is orbited by a single electron. The uranium atom, the largest atom found on earth, has ninety-two protons orbited by ninety-two electrons.

A proton is the positively charged particle. The name was suggested by Rutherford in 1920 and was taken from a Greek word meaning "first" or "primary particle." The number of protons in every element corresponds to what is known as an element's *atomic number.* Thus hydrogen, with one proton, has an atomic number of 1, while helium, with two protons, is numbered 2. Sodium is 11, krypton 36, lead 82, and uranium, with ninety-two protons, has an atomic number of 92. An element has been discovered on earth for every number between one and ninety-two, while atoms with more than ninety-two protons have been artificially made by scientists under special conditions.

In addition to protons and electrons, several other particles have been discovered in the atom, but only one needs to be mentioned here: the neutron. The neutron was discovered in 1932, but its existence had been predicted earlier. Nuclear physicists knew, for instance, that the element helium, with an atomic number of 2 had an *atomic weight* * of 4. The only way to account for the discrepancy was to theorize the existence of two more particles in the helium nucleus. These particles would have the same weight as protons, but they would have no electric charge.

The existence of neutrons also helped to explain another question that bothered nuclear scientists. The question arose when it was discovered that one element, like lead, could come in a variety of forms. Each form of lead had the same atomic number—82—but differed in atomic weight. With the discovery of neutrons, it was easy to account for the different weights of lead atoms. The difference lay in the number of neutrons in the nucleus of the lead atom. Some lead atoms had a larger number of neutrons, others had a smaller number. The different forms of an element were called *isotopes,* from the Greek words meaning "equal place." Each isotope of an element held an "equal place," or an equal number of protons, but varied from the other isotopes of the same element as to the number of neutrons contained in the nucleus.

Let us take a close look at one element—uranium—in or-

* Atomic weight is the weight of a representative atom of an element relative to the weight of an atom of carbon-12 which is given a value of 12. Thus the atomic weight of hydrogen is 1.0080 while that of uranium is 238.029.

der to understand what has been said. As noted earlier, uranium has an atomic number of 92. This means that there are 92 protons in the uranium nucleus. At the same time, every uranium atom has 92 electrons, so that the positive charges of the protons are balanced by the negative charges of the electrons. Uranium has several isotopes. These are abbreviated scientifically as U-233, U-235, and U-238. U-233 has an atomic weight of 233. By subtracting the number of protons from this number, we can find the number of neutrons in the uranium isotope 233; 233 minus 92 equals 141. U-233 contains 141 neutrons. Similarly, U-235 contains 143 neutrons (235 − 92 = 143), and U-238 has 146 neutrons.

THE POWER OF THE ATOM

As the secrets of the atom began to unfold, it became obvious to many scientists that the atom must contain a great deal of energy. First was the question of what held the atom together. If the atom contained a number of positive and negative charges, what kept these charges separate? Positive and negative charges attract one another and it would seem logical to assume that the protons and electrons in an atom would be drawn to one another—unless some strong force acted to stabilize the atom and keep the protons and electrons in their proper places.

Similarly, like charges repel one another. Positively charged electrical particles should reject other positive particles and negatively charged particles should reject other negative particles. Yet the positively charged protons were bound together in the atomic nucleus. Here too some great force must be at work holding the nucleus together.

Furthermore, the size and structure of the atom also hinted at extraordinary power. An atom is exceedingly small yet it contains particles even smaller than the atom. If we can imagine an enlarged hydrogen atom, it would look something like this. At the center is the nucleus, a single proton, the size of a marble. Forty-six meters (150 feet) away from the proton is a single electron whirling around the proton an estimated seven million billion times every second. The single electron is 1,840 times smaller than the marble, yet the electron and proton remain combined in the hydrogen atom.

The scientist who first defined the nature of the energy in the atom was Albert Einstein. In 1905, Einstein—who was only twenty-six at the time—published what is probably the best-known equation of all time: $E = mc^2$. Energy is equal to the mass multiplied by the square of the speed of light. This meant that mass could be converted into energy * and energy into mass. Since the square of the speed of light is an enormous number (186,000 miles per second times 186,000 miles per second equals 34,596 million), a small amount of mass will yield a great deal of energy. Indeed, it can be shown, according to Einstein's equation, that the energy contained in a lump of sugar would generate enough power to keep an electric heater going for 5,708 years. Even the small mass of an atom, when multiplied by the square of the speed of light, yields an extraordinary amount of energy.

Einstein was way ahead of his time. It was not until 1932 that experimental evidence confirmed the truth of his equation. Confirmation was provided by the work of two English physicists, J. D. Cockcroft and E. T. S. Walton, who were the first scientists to split an atom by artificial means. Cockcroft and Walton worked with the element lithium, with an atomic number of 3 and an atomic weight of 7. (This meant that the nucleus of the lithium atom they used had three protons and four neutrons [3 + 4 = 7].)

Cockcroft and Walton hit a lithium 7 nucleus with a loose proton. At first, the loose proton was absorbed by the lithium nucleus, but then the nucleus split into two alpha particles.

The experiment proved that an atom of one element could

* Mass should not be confused with weight. The weight of an object is the force that gravity exerts on the mass. The mass of an object does not change. If you would travel to Jupiter, your weight would increase a great deal, due to the greater pull of gravity. Your mass, however, would remain the same.

be changed into something quite different. It also proved Einstein's equation, because when the energy released during the splitting of the lithium atom was measured, it corresponded to Einstein's predictions. The amount of energy released, however, was not of practical significance. It would take several more years of experimentation before scientists developed a means to split an atom and achieve a full yield of the energy inside.

It is difficult to overestimate the achievements of the men and women who were the early pioneers in atomic science. In a relatively short time—roughly between 1895 and 1930 —they had undermined earlier atomic theories, uncovered the nature and structure of the atom, and discovered its enormous power. Later generations of physicists and engineers would refine and greatly expand the field of nuclear energy, but they nevertheless owed a great deal to the work of the pioneers, who set them in the right direction and made the basic discoveries.

CHAPTER 3
NUCLEAR ENERGY AND NUCLEAR REACTORS

It was the discovery of the neutron in 1932 that made the splitting of the atom a far more easy task for science to accomplish. The neutron has the same mass as a proton, but it has no electrical charge. It is therefore a better "bullet" to fire at a nucleus, because there is no chance that it will be repelled by the positively charged protons in the center of the atom.

Soon after the discovery of the neutron, the Italian physicist Enrico Fermi began to experiment with its use as an "atom splitter." Fermi and his associates bombarded the nuclei of several kinds of elements with neutrons and found that slower-moving neutrons were better at splitting nuclei than fast-moving ones. When they fired their loose, or free, neutrons at the nuclei of uranium atoms, they found that the atoms divided into new elements, which were no longer uranium, but were still radioactive and emitted beta particles.

The products of the divided uranium atom were later identified as the elements barium and krypton. Uranium, with an atomic number of 92, had split into barium, with an atomic number of 56, and krypton, whose number is 36 ($56 + 36 = 92$). There are more than thirty ways in which a uranium atom can divide, but this was the first to be recorded. From Stockholm, Lise Meitner, a German scientist who had fled the

Nazism of her native country, suggested that the additional neutron had caused the unstable uranium nucleus to split and form atoms of more stable elements—since barium and krypton were recognized for their stability.

Meitner's suggestion was significant because it implied that a great deal of energy was released when a uranium atom split. The reason for this release of energy is not difficult to understand. The elements in the middle range of atomic numbers, like barium and krypton, have what is known as the greatest binding energy of all the elements. This means that the nuclei of these elements are relatively stable and firmly "packed," because a great deal of energy has gone into their formation. In order to pack protons and neutrons into the stable nuclei of barium and krypton, the uranium atom would have to release a great deal of energy when it split.

But Meitner's suggestion was also significant for another reason. When uranium split into barium and krypton, a number of neutrons were released. A barium atom contains 82 neutrons and a krypton atom 47, for a total of 129. Since the uranium atom had 146 neutrons, this means that 17 were now free and loose (18, if the "bullet" neutron that split the uranium atom is taken into consideration). These 18 neutrons could strike other nuclei, releasing more free neutrons and greater amounts of energy.

Another way to look at the release of energy by an atomic nucleus is to consider the radioactive decay process. In Chapter 2, we looked at Rutherford and Stoddy's theory of "radioactive disintegration." According to this theory, unstable, radioactive elements, like radium, continue to decay and re-form until some stable form of element is reached. In the process, they release energy, as protons and neutrons are packed into a nucleus that has stability and that is no longer radioactive.

Radium undergoes a number of changes before it becomes lead. First, it releases an alpha particle and becomes radon. The release of yet another alpha particle produces polonium. After nine more decay processes, the element thallium is reached. The thallium releases a beta particle and becomes the stable element lead. This steady release of energy accounts for a piece of radium being warmer than its surroundings. The energy is generated over a long period of time—thousands of years—and is a spontaneous, natural process. The splitting of a uranium atom by artificial means, however, releases a great deal of energy all at once. The move from an unstable element to a stable element is only a matter of seconds.

WORLD WAR II

Research into nuclear energy was greatly stimulated by World War II. In the early years of the war, Albert Einstein, who had left Germany to come to the United States, warned President Franklin D. Roosevelt in a letter that science had reached the stage where it could produce a nuclear bomb —a bomb that would be far more powerful than any ever made. The government began to fund the research of the country's leading physicists whose work became top secret and who were placed under the supervision of the military. The aim of the program—which was called the Manhattan Project—was to solve all the problems that remained in learning how to split the atom with the greatest possible yield of energy. The Project was to create a nuclear bomb before the Germans, our enemies, produced one.

One of the first problems the physicists encountered concerned uranium isotopes. Uranium samples contained two important isotopes (there were also others present, but these were less significant): uranium 235 and uranium 238. Of the two isotopes, only one, U-235, readily undergoes nuclear fission (splits), when bombarded by a free neutron. The problem was compounded by the fact that U-238, which does not fission, forms most of the uranium ore present in the world. For every 1 atom of U-235, there are 140 atoms of U-238. Clearly, fission would be more efficient if uranium samples were enriched with a greater amount of U-235.

There was also another side to the dilemma of the isotopes. As we saw earlier, Fermi discovered that slow neutrons produced fission better than fast neutrons. But when a slow free neutron strikes a U-235 nucleus, the neutrons that are released travel at fast speeds. These fast neutrons are quickly absorbed by the nuclei of U-238 and are then no longer available to strike U-235 nuclei. As a result, the chain reaction comes to a stop before much energy has been released. The problem for the physicists to solve, in addition to the problem of uranium enrichment with more atoms of U-235, was how to moderate the speeds of newly escaped free neutrons so that they were slow enough to strike U-235 nuclei and split them.

Through trial and error, scientists learned how to enrich uranium with U-235. It was a difficult process, since U-235 and U-238 cannot be separated by chemical means, but must rely on more complex and sophisticated methods of separation. But finally uranium samples were produced that contained a sufficient percentage of U-235 to assure that a nuclear chain reaction will take place, if the circumstances are right.

The second problem—the need to slow down fast neutrons—was solved by the use of a moderator. The scientists who worked on the Manhattan Project knew that certain light elements, such as helium, carbon, and beryllium, did not absorb fast neutrons easily, but caused them to bounce away and thereby slow down their speeds. By adding pure graphite—which is carbon—to an enriched sample of uranium, an ideal situation for a chain reaction could be created. The fast neutrons that escaped from a split U-235 nucleus would now strike carbon nuclei, be slowed down sufficiently so that they could strike other U-235 nuclei, and sustain the chain reaction.

A final problem was known as critical size. If the uranium sample were too small or wrongly shaped, too many free neutrons would escape from the surface of the sample and be lost to the chain reaction. The physicists therefore had to determine the size and shape the uranium had to take before the right number of neutrons were held within the sample in order to maintain fission. When the problem of

A sketch of the first atomic pile as it appeared
at the University of Chicago in 1942. This
drawing, made in 1946, is based on the physical
measurements of the reactor, and the recollections
of the scientists who worked on the project.

MELVIN A. MILLER '46

critical size had been solved, it was believed that the right time had come to test what had been learned about nuclear energy and to see if a chain reaction could be sustained.

A first attempt under the guidance of Enrico Fermi and the Hungarian physicist Leo Szilard at Columbia University in New York City failed. But the effort had come close to success and no one felt discouraged. The Columbia University group was reassembled at the University of Chicago. All through 1942 work proceeded on the project. Materials were carefully selected and prepared. An "atomic pile" was constructed in laboratories beneath the university's squash courts. By the end of the year, the scientists were ready to test their pile and on December 2, the world's first self-sustaining chain reaction took place. The atomic age was born.

The historic atomic pile at the University of Chicago consisted of a lattice-work of purified graphite and uranium. Bricks of graphite were used to separate small lumps of uranium metal placed at regular intervals throughout the pile. The carbon in the graphite slowed down the neutrons that escaped from the U-235.

In order to control the chain reaction and make certain that a sudden release of energy did not result in an explosion, the scientists at Chicago inserted cadmium rods into the atomic pile. Cadmium is an element that will absorb free neutrons, but is not changed by them and will not undergo fission. The rods were situated so that they could be moved in and out of the pile. When they were in the pile, the cadmium would slow down the fission process and bring it to a halt; when they were removed from the pile, free neutrons would continue to split U-235 nuclei and release new free neutrons that would in turn split new U-235 nuclei.

The successful chain reaction sustained below the squash courts at the University of Chicago pointed in two directions: toward the development of a nuclear bomb and toward the nuclear reactor. While World War II continued, however, primary emphasis was understandably placed on the bomb. Throughout 1943 and 1944, an all-out effort was made to solve all the problems that remained and to produce the most efficient bomb possible. By 1945 those problems had been ironed out. A nuclear weapon was successfully tested in New Mexico and a few days later, in early August, atomic bombs were dropped on Hiroshima and Nagasaki, Japan.

The power of the bombs shocked the world and helped to bring the war to a close. Hiroshima and Nagasaki were leveled and hundreds of thousands of people were killed or made ill by the bombs and the radiation they produced. The energy released by the bombs had been enormous. If allowed to undergo spontaneous fission, .45 kilograms (1 pound) of U-235 has the explosive force of 9,090 metric tons (10,000 *tons*) of TNT. This means that pound for pound, U-235 has an explosive force twenty million times more powerful than TNT.

But other facts about the explosions were even more extraordinary. The bomb that destroyed Nagasaki contained plutonium, an element discovered during the war that was highly radioactive and underwent a fission process similar to U-235. "Fat Man," as the Nagasaki bomb was nicknamed by its makers, held several kilograms of plutonium, yet the amount of plutonium that produced the explosion amounted to about one gram (.035 ounces)—one-third the weight of a penny.

THE DEVELOPMENT OF
THE NUCLEAR REACTOR

The development of the nuclear reactor paralleled the development of the bomb. Invented in 1943, the first reactor was designed from the principles learned at the atomic pile at the University of Chicago. The purpose of the reactor was to take the heat generated in the atomic pile by the radioactive fuel and transform this heat into another type of energy. The energy in the reactor would be carefully moderated and controlled so that there would be no explosion and

On a July morning in 1957, the fireball from one of the largest atomic devices ever exploded in the United States rose over an atomic test site in Nevada.

so that a steady amount of power was made available to drive a motor or produce electricity.

One of the earliest uses mentioned for the reactor was in submarines. A nuclear-powered submarine had a definite advantage over a conventional submarine. It could remain submerged for longer periods of time, since it would not have to refuel as often. At the end of the war, the American government began a program geared to produce a nuclear submarine which culminated with the launching of the *Nautilus* in 1955. During this period, many technical problems involved in the construction of reactors were solved and the basic reactor design evolved. When President Eisenhower announced his Atoms for Peace program in 1953, reactor development had already reached the point where the commercial generation of electricity by nuclear power could not be far away.

The basic design of a reactor is simple, but the technical and engineering problems involved in its construction are difficult and highly sophisticated. In order to construct a reactor, we need a *fuel* that has been properly enriched and purified, a *moderator* to slow down the fast neutrons that escape from a splitting nucleus, and *control rods* of some material that will absorb neutrons without reacting to them. We also need a *coolant* that helps to cool the fuel and at the same time transfers the heat generated in the reactor to the *heat exchangers,* which, in turn, drive the turbines that generate electricity. And, finally, we need a *safety shield* to protect the staff and operators of the reactor from radioactive contamination.

From the fuel to the safety shield, the reactor must be put together with the utmost care to assure its absolute safety and reliability. Each part of the reactor presents its own hazards and problems.

1. Fuel. The fuel is usually manufactured in pellets and must be of the best quality. In addition, the fuel pellets must be coated, or "clad," in a material that will protect them from the reactor coolant, in which the fuel will be submerged. A reaction between the fuel and the coolant would damage the fuel and might also lead to a blockage of the reactor's functions.

The cladding, or substance that coats the fuel, must be a good conductor of heat so that no energy is lost. It must not absorb neutrons from the fuel (if it did, the chain reaction would come to a stop), and it must be able to withstand very high temperatures without damage. Scientists have found that one of the best claddings is an alloy of the element zirconium. But even the best claddings must be checked from time to time for wear, corrosion, or other possible damage.

2. The Moderator. The principal problem involved with the moderator is purity. When graphite is used, as it was in the first atomic pile, the graphite must be as free as possible from any contamination. Impure graphite would tend to absorb free neutrons and lower the efficiency of the reactor. Other materials have also been used as moderators, including ordinary water, heavy water, and the element beryllium.

3. The Control Rods. The control rods are a very important part of the reactor. Without them, the chain reaction would get out of hand and probably explode.* The rods must be made of a material that readily absorbs free neutrons and that does not react to these neutrons. The elements cadmium and boron are frequently used as control rod material. In order to be fashioned into rods, they are combined with aluminum or steel. It is important that the control rods are always ready to drop into the reactor core when needed. A malfunction in the mechanism that raises and lowers the

---

* A conventional reactor cannot cause a nuclear explosion similar to an exploding atomic bomb. But an explosion at a reactor could crack the reactor wall or lead to other damage to the plant that would result in the release of radioactivity.

The reactor core of the Duane Arnold Energy Center, near Palo, Iowa. With the reactor head removed, fuel can be lowered into a grid in the reactor vessel. When functioning, the reactor vessel will also contain control rods and water.

rods would be very serious and could result in a great deal of damage.

4. The Coolant. The coolant carries the heat produced in the reactor core to the heat exchangers where it is transferred to the system that drives the turbine engine. A coolant must have two essential properties. It must be a very good conductor of heat so that little heat is lost in the transfer of energy, and it should absorb as few free neutrons as possible.

Several kinds of coolants have been used in reactors, including various gases, ordinary water, heavy water, organic liquids, and liquid metals. Carbon dioxide (a gas) is inexpensive, but it is not very efficient and it reacts at high temperatures with the graphite moderator. Heavy water is very expensive. Ordinary water must be used under high pressure or it will turn to steam. Liquid metals, such as sodium or an alloy of sodium and potassium, tend to become radioactive and will react violently with water, should the reactor develop a leak.

One of the most dangerous accidents that can happen to a reactor is known as a loss-of-coolant accident, or a LOCA. This happens when the pumps that circulate the coolant through the reactor core cease to function. In a very short time, the reactor could overheat, resulting in damage that could lead to leakage of radioactive material. As we shall see in the next chapter, nuclear scientists and engineers have created an elaborate series of safeguards to make certain that a LOCA does not occur or to bring a LOCA that has already begun quickly under control.

5. The Heat Exchangers. Heat exchangers must be strong and durable and able to resist high pressures. A highly sophisticated procedure has been developed to manufacture heat exchangers that will withstand all foreseeable problems that might arise. It is important that the heat exchangers function well, because radioactivity in the coolant could reach other parts of the reactor. In the heat exchangers, the coolant, heated from its contact with the reactor core, heats water which turns to steam to drive the turbines. When a reactor is constructed, elaborate efforts are made to see that the heat exchanger is fitted and welded properly, to prevent any loss of radiation.

6. The Safety Shield. Since several forms of radioactivity and radioactive elements are produced in the reactor core when it is in operation, the men and women who work in the plant must be protected from contamination. This is done by a safety shield—usually of thick concrete—that absorbs even the most penetrating types of radiation. Since openings in the shielding have to be made to allow for the flow of coolant and other reactor parts, caution must be taken to see that there is no leakage of radioactivity from these openings. To create an even greater degree of safety, a second shielding is placed around the first. Often this second shielding is more than 1.8 meters (6 feet) thick.

TYPES OF REACTORS
Many reactor types have been developed since 1943, but only a few have been considered efficient and reliable enough to be tested and put into production. Most of these reactors follow the basic design we have outlined above, but vary in the kind of fuel, coolant, or moderator used, or in some other way from the basic plan.

1. Pressurized-Water Reactors (PWR). The PWR is now the most common type of reactor found in the United States. It was developed from the small reactors used in atomic submarines. The PWR uses ordinary pure water as both moderator and coolant. The water is kept under great pressure so that it will not turn to steam under the high temperatures reached in the reactor core (about 315° C, or 600° F). Since large PWRs produce electricity more cheaply than small PWRs, PWRs are now usually large undertakings. An example of a PWR is the 1,000-megawatt (MW) plant of the Consolidated Edison Company near Buchanan, in Westchester County, New York. (One megawatt is equal to one

Schematic of a Pressurized–Water Reactor Power Plant

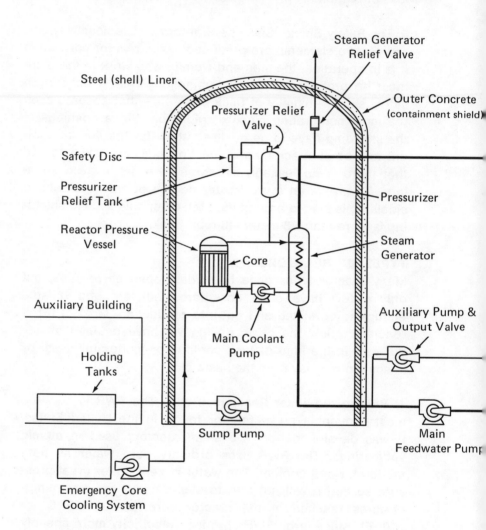

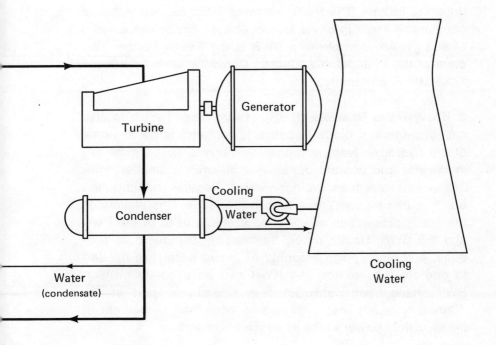

Turbine

Generator

Condenser

Cooling
Water

Water
(condensate)

Cooling
Water

———— Primary System
━━━━ Secondary System

million watts.) The damaged reactor at Three Mile Island in Pennsylvania is also a PWR.

2. Boiling-Water Reactors (BWR). In the BWR, cool water is placed in the reactor core, where it is heated to boiling under high pressure. The steam that rises in the top of the reactor is carried to the turbine which generates electricity. The BWR thus eliminates the double delivery system of the PWR, where the coolant heats a second supply of water to drive the turbine. The BWR, however, must be larger than a comparable PWR in order to produce an equivalent amount of energy. An example of a BWR is the Peach Bottom Two plant of the Philadelphia Electric Company which produces 1,065 MW of electricity.

3. Heavy-Water Reactors (HWR). Heavy water (which is also called deuterium oxide because it contains large amounts of the hydrogen isotope deuterium) serves as an excellent moderator and coolant because it absorbs a smaller number of neutrons than ordinary water. Regular, nonenriched uranium can be used as a fuel in the HWR. This eliminates the costly production of enriched uranium used in the PWR and the BWR. Heavy water, however, is expensive to produce, and since large amounts of heavy water are needed to operate the reactor, the HWR can be a costly project. HWRs have been constructed in Canada as part of the "Candu system." They now supply more than 14 percent of the electrical power in the province of Ontario.

4. High-Temperature Gas-Cooled Reactors (HTGR). In an HTGR, a gas, usually helium or carbon dioxide, is used as the coolant. Graphite (carbon) is used as the moderator. Helium and carbon dioxide allow higher temperatures to be reached in the reactor core than can be reached when ordinary water or heavy water are used as coolants. As a result, HTGRs can produce electricity more efficiently than other types of reactors. HTGRs are popular in Europe, but have also been constructed in the United States. An example is the Fort Saint Vrain power station in Colorado.

5. Organic-Cooled Reactors (OCR). In the OCR, an organic liquid is used as the coolant. The organic liquid allows the use of a natural, nonenriched uranium as fuel (as in the HWR) and can reach high temperatures (as in the HTGR). At the same time, an OCR does not require the high pressures needed in the cores of other reactors. Organic liquids make cheaper coolants than heavy water, but are high absorbers of free neutrons and are flammable. At present, there is an OCR in operation at Whiteshell, Manitoba.

6. Breeder Reactors. Each of the reactor types we have looked at until now have the disadvantage of using up their fuel. New fuel—whether enriched uranium or ordinary uranium—must be supplied from time to time in order to keep the reactor active. Since there is a finite supply of uranium in the world, these reactors would at some point reach a time when uranium becomes scarce and expensive. The reactors would cease the production of electricity, because their supply of fuel had been exhausted.

There is another kind of reactor, however, called the breeder reactor, that produces fuel as it generates heat and energy. Indeed, the breeder reactor "breeds" more fuel than it uses up. It can be compared to a car that starts out one morning and is driven throughout the day. In the evening, the tank contains more gasoline than it did at the start of the journey.

Because of its amazing properties, the breeder reactor has been part of the "nuclear future" envisioned by the nuclear industry from the very beginning. The breeder offered a means to avoid the eventual exhaustion of the world's uranium supply for a long period of time. One breeder reactor, situated at a site with several conventional reactors, could manufacture the fuel that would keep those reactors in operation.

The fuel used in a breeder reactor is plutonium, an element that exists on earth only as an artificially produced, manmade substance. Unlike U-235, plutonium does not need slow neutrons in order for its nucleus to fission. Therefore, there is no need for a moderator to slow down the free neutrons. A breeder reactor can be much smaller than a reactor whose fuel needs a moderator.

The plutonium core of the breeder reactor is surrounded by rods of uranium 238, the most common isotope of uranium. When the reactor is in operation, these rods of U-238 will be converted into plutonium. What happens is this: When a free neutron from the plutonium core is absorbed by a nucleus of a U-238 atom, an isotope of uranium known as U-239 is formed.

Uranium 239 is a highly unstable form of uranium and soon re-forms to produce the element neptunium, yielding an electron in the process. Neptunium, with an atomic number of 93, is the next element above uranium, just as the planet Neptune is the first planet beyond Uranus in the solar system. Neptunium is also unstable and changes to plutonium (named for Pluto, the planet beyond Neptune), plus another electron.

What is remarkable about this process is that for every four atoms of plutonium that are used up in the core of the breeder, five new plutonium atoms are formed from the uranium 238. The primary breeder design is known as the *liquid-metal-cooled fast breeder reactor* (LMFBR). It is called a "fast" breeder because it has no need of a moderator. The liquid metal used as a coolant is liquid sodium. A breeder will frequently have a complicated set of heat exchangers in order to keep the liquid sodium away from any chance contact with water, with which it would react violently.

Breeder reactors have been built and operated successfully. Indeed, the first electricity generated by any reactor was produced by a small, experimental breeder in Idaho in 1951. But the breeder reactor has yet to prove itself economically as a practical and inexpensive way to produce fuel and electricity. There are several technical problems involved that have not been solved, not least of which is the difficulty in slowing down the breeder.

Since the breeder reactor uses fast neutrons, there is less time to react in case of accident than there is in a standard reactor using slow neutrons. At present, the LMFBRs are in an experimental stage in the United States, with plans to put them in operation sometime in the 1990s. In France and Great Britain, however, breeder reactors have been constructed that deliver 250 MW of electricity and there are plans to construct plants two or three times larger.

From the discovery of the atomic nucleus and its powers through the construction of nuclear bombs and reactors, science has come a long way in a short period of time. The achievements in the field of nuclear energy have been spectacular and have given the men and women responsible for them a sense of exhilaration and a feeling that any problem can be solved, if the right expertise is applied to it.

These feelings of exhilaration and achievement are in large part responsible for the optimism and confidence many nuclear advocates have when they approach the question of nuclear energy. Since nuclear science has confronted difficult questions in the past and successfully answered them, they feel it will undoubtedly solve the perplexing problems of the present and the future.

CHAPTER 4
THE CASE FOR
NUCLEAR ENERGY

The advocates of nuclear energy come from many walks of life. Some are scientists and engineers who have intimate knowledge of nuclear physics and the problems involved in nuclear technology. Others are men and women prominent in business and government who believe that the world's energy crisis can only be solved by continued development of nuclear power sources. But whatever their backgrounds, the advocates argue that nuclear energy is desirable because it is relatively inexpensive, safe, and pollution-free when compared to the other energy sources now available.

THE ECONOMICS OF
NUCLEAR ENERGY

The proponents of nuclear energy do not claim that nuclear power will be cheap. On the contrary, they recognize that nuclear power has frequently proved to be very costly and that it will continue to rise in price, like almost everything else. What they do argue, however, is that nuclear power is economically competitive with any other source of power.

Oil and natural gas are out of the question because of their growing scarcity and rising prices. Solar energy cannot be relied upon at this time to supply the amount of power the world will need in the immediate future, because solar technology is still in its infancy. The only viable alternative to nuclear power is coal, and when nuclear power is compared to coal, the advocates claim, nuclear power is easily the winner.

There have been several studies that show nuclear power to be cheaper than power derived from coal, but one of the most interesting appeared in the prestigious magazine *Science* (August 18, 1978), the publication of the American Association for the Advancement of Science. Entitled "Economics of Nuclear Power" and written by two nuclear research engineers and analysts for the Consolidated Edison Company, the study compared the operation of six large nuclear plants and six large coal-fired plants owned by Consolidated Edison.

The conclusions were clear. The nuclear plants saved customers about 10 percent on their utility bills in 1977 alone when compared with the plants that used coal. The authors concluded that the advantage of nuclear power over coal was likely to continue, yielding further savings in the future. These conclusions were similar to the conclusions of other articles by reputable scientists and engineers that have appeared in the same journal.

The authors also point out that nuclear energy can prove economical in ways that are not immediately detectable. Increased use of nuclear power, for instance, will tend to free the United States from dependence on oil that is used to produce electricity. This means that the country will have to import less oil in the future, making it less subject to the demands of the oil-producing nations.

Similarly, an increased use of nuclear power will help to preserve the coal supplies that remain in the earth, as well as the dwindling supplies of oil and natural gas. This will make more coal, oil, and natural gas available for the production of plastics and chemicals and for the many other nonenergy functions they serve. Otherwise, the costs of these products will rise enormously, as the resources they are made from grow more expensive.

Finally, the proponents of nuclear energy mention one

other economic advantage that will come with nuclear development. When breeder reactors are built on a large scale —probably sometime in the 1990s—there will be a new source of fuel to operate reactors. Breeders are able to unlock up to 60 percent of the energy stored in uranium, compared to the 1 to 5 percent that is released by conventional reactors. This will make nuclear energy one of the most efficient sources of power and will provide large supplies of relatively cheap fuel to power the new reactors of the future.

THE SAFETY OF
NUCLEAR ENERGY

The proponents of nuclear energy say it is safer than other forms of energy. This is particularly true in the case of coal, the only fuel that offers nuclear power competition at this time. In an article in *American Scientist* (May–June, 1976) entitled "Nuclear Power—Compared to What?" David J. Rose, a professor of nuclear engineering at the Massachusetts Institute of Technology, and two other authors looked at the hazards of coal and nuclear energy and opted for the safety of nuclear energy.

First, Rose and his colleagues found that coal mining results in three times as many deaths as does the mining of uranium. But the greatest danger to coal miners was a long-term, debilitating illness known as miner's lung, which is caused by breathing coal dust. Tens of thousands of American miners suffer from miner's lung (or black lung, as it is also called) and are incapable of work. There is no comparable illness that afflicts uranium miners, not even illnesses due to exposure to radiation.

Furthermore, Rose showed that the burning of coal in power plants releases several kinds of pollutants into the atmosphere, including sulphur oxides, nitrogen oxides, and trace metals. In recent years, the government has placed severe restrictions on coal-burning plants, and as a result, pollution from coal has been greatly reduced. But a percentage of the tiniest pollutant particles still reaches the outside world, and these tiny particles are the most dangerous to human health and to other forms of life because they are able to penetrate the recesses of the lungs.

As a result of the current energy crisis, some of the more stringent restrictions on coal-burning have been lifted. This means that a great deal more of the hazardous materials now reach the atmosphere. A study of these pollutants by the Environmental Protection Agency (EPA), a division of the federal government, shows that they are potentially far more dangerous than radiation that might leak from a nuclear reactor. The chief problems they can produce are chronic respiratory illnesses and aggravation of heart disease —diseases that can afflict thousands of people who live near coal-burning plants.

A final problem associated with the burning of coal that is mentioned by Rose is the long-term warming of the earth's atmosphere. This is caused by the carbon dioxide released into the atmosphere when the plant is in operation. The additional carbon dioxide will create a "greenhouse effect" which will warm the atmosphere gradually. A change of one or two degrees in temperature could trigger widespread alterations in climate and weather, alterations that could not be controlled and that could prove disastrous for crop-growing areas and raise other unwelcome problems.

With these facts in mind, Rose and his colleagues ask why a "Fossil Fuel Regulatory Commission" has not been established. This commission could oversee the hazards of coal, just as the Atomic Energy Commission and the Nuclear Regulatory Commission oversee the hazards of nuclear energy. They conclude that the nuclear industry has unfairly been required to follow extremely rigid standards of safety, while the coal industry—which they have shown to be more dangerous to health than nuclear power—has been relatively free of regulation and safety restrictions.

THE HAZARDS OF
NUCLEAR REACTORS

Rose and his coauthors raise a point that has irritated nuclear proponents for some time. Nuclear advocates believe that the nuclear industry has been the victim of public fears

49]

and ignorance about nuclear energy. These fears have tended to make nuclear energy seem far more dangerous than it really is. They may arise from concern about nuclear explosions or worry about the hazards of radiation. But whatever their origin, the nuclear advocates argue that they can be dispelled, if the public will take a close, impartial, and scientific look at nuclear energy. It will then see that enormous efforts have been made to construct reactors safely and to minimize any accident that might occur.

The two chief threats posed by a reactor are radiation leakage and some form of accident that might cause the reactor to explode, sending radioactive debris throughout the area. Nuclear scientists have carefully analyzed the operation of reactors in order to locate each spot where these threats might occur. An elaborate system of inspections and safeguards has been developed that must be followed by every reactor licensed by the federal government. According to nuclear proponents, this system of inspections and safeguards has proved so thorough that the chances of a disaster are very slim.

Routine emissions from nuclear reactors. Most of the radioactivity found in a reactor is confined to the reactor core and its immediate area. Some, however, is allowed to escape into the atmosphere as part of the routine functioning of the reactor. These routine emissions include small amounts of radioactive iodine and krypton in gaseous form. The amount of these materials released is not significant. Nuclear experts estimate that if there were enough reactors in the United States to produce all the electricity the country needed, the total amount of radiation from the released iodine and krypton would not be harmful to human life.

Another possible source of pollution from the reactor is tritium. Tritium is an isotope of hydrogen that readily combines with ordinary hydrogen in water and cannot be separated. When water is returned to the river from the reactor, the tritium flows with it. However, it is estimated that if all our power were nuclear, the average person would receive only a small dosage of radiation from this source.

50]

Indeed, when all the possible exposures to radiation due to routine emissions are added together, the average American would receive only 0.23 millirems (mrem) * of radiation per year. This figure is far lower than the amount of radiation an individual receives from natural radiation in the air and earth (130 mrem per year). It is also lower than the average exposure due to dental and medical X rays, which is about 70 mrem per year. With these facts in mind, nuclear experts have concluded that routine emissions offer no danger to public health, as long as the emissions are kept very low.

Power plant accidents. Potentially more dangerous than the problem of routine emissions is a reactor accident. If an accident occurred at a major nuclear plant, the damage could be great. Since the radioactivity in a reactor is primarily confined to the reactor core, the most dangerous accidents would involve damage to the core and its operations. Temperatures within the reactor could reach as high as 2,760° C (5,000° F) and at this temperature a meltdown, described in chapter 1, could take place.

The most likely cause of a meltdown is a "loss-of-coolant accident," or LOCA, resulting from a leak in the cooling water-system. Since the water in a PWR (pressurized-water reactor) or a BWR (boiling-water reactor) is kept under high pressure, any leak or rupture in the system would cause the coolant to escape from the reactor in the form of steam at a tremendous rate. The reactor core would then be left without any coolant. Without the coolant, which also acts as a moderator in the PWR and BWR, the number of slow neutrons available for fission would decrease and the chain reaction would come to a halt.

The chain reaction would stop, but radioactive decay of the fuel would continue. The heat generated in the normal radioactive decay of the fuel would be great enough to cause a meltdown. If the fuel in the PWR were left without

* A rem is a unit used to measure biological damage done by radiation. A millirem is one one-thousandth of a rem.

a coolant for forty-five seconds, and possibly even thirty seconds, the reactor would be headed for a meltdown (a BWR could be left without coolant for as much as three to five minutes). Complete meltdown of the reactor could follow in about thirty minutes, and in an hour, the fuel would melt through the reactor vessel.

Nuclear scientists and engineers have realized these grave problems for many years and have taken steps to avoid them. First, all materials that go into the construction of a reactor are closely analyzed and inspected during their manufacture, in order to eliminate any flaws or imperfections. Once the reactor has been built, its structure is thoroughly tested before it can go into operation. These tests include X-ray inspection of all welds, ultrasonic tests of materials to reveal imperfections, and magnetic-particle inspections. Finally, all reactors in operation are periodically shut down so that extensive visual and ultrasonic examinations can be made to uncover any flaws that have appeared during the stress of nuclear activity.

Since it is possible that a reactor might malfunction between inspections, other safeguards have also been developed to prevent or minimize a loss-of-coolant accident. Sensitive detectors have been placed in strategic spots to warn the operators of the reactor if steam has begun to leak or if the amount of radioactivity near the reactor is higher than it should be. These detectors would allow the operators to shut down the reactor so that repairs could be made.

Another method that will prevent a LOCA from resulting in a meltdown is the "emergency core cooling system," or ECCS. Under this system, water is quickly pumped into the reactor to replace the lost coolant. The ECCS is complex, but the scientists and engineers who designed it are confident that it has a 99-percent chance of delivering water in case of a loss-of-coolant accident.

Finally, nuclear proponents remind us that a reactor is contained within a structure made of very thick and strong concrete that is lined with steel plate. The container is made to withstand enormous pressures, and would greatly reduce the seriousness of any accident that might occur.

Inspection systems, sensitive steam and radiation detectors, the ECCS, and concrete shielding have greatly reduced the dangers of a loss-of-coolant accident. But what are the remaining chances of a nuclear plant disaster? Very slim indeed, the advocates of nuclear energy answer. Norman Rasmussen, a professor at the Massachusetts Institute of Technology, estimates that a meltdown could happen only once in every fifty years. Since Rasmussen bases his estimation on the assumption that all our electricity will be derived from nuclear energy (which will take at least four hundred large reactors), this means that only one reactor out of four hundred will meltdown within a fifty-year period.

This accident, according to Rasmussen, would result in ten deaths from acute radiation sickness, five hundred eventual deaths from cancer, and would result in $300 million worth of damage—for the most part cleanup and evacuation costs. The worst possible accident, Rasmussen concluded, would result in thirty-five hundred fatalities, forty-five thousand cancer deaths, and cost $14 billion. But the chances of this kind of accident were so slim that it could happen only once in a million years.

These figures sound horrible and completely unacceptable, but they must be put into perspective. Nuclear energy is risky and carries the chance that accidents can occur. But risky as nuclear energy is, it is far less dangerous, say the nuclear proponents, than other forms of energy. There are hydroelectric dams whose failure could result in 200,000 immediate deaths—and the failure of a dam is statistically far more likely than a major nuclear accident. In addition, there are situations where the transportation of liquified natural gas could result in 100,000 deaths, and these too are more likely than nuclear accidents. And earlier in this chapter, we saw how coal-burning plants present a greater threat to health than nuclear plants.

Any form of energy we use, the nuclear advocates conclude, can result in death and disaster, but nuclear energy can be shown to be the safest form now available to us. Besides, the nuclear industry has a good record. Naval reactors have operated for many years without a meltdown or other serious accident. Even the much publicized accident at Three Mile Island can be viewed as a success for the nuclear industry, since nuclear expertise was able to control a situation that could have become much worse.

Transportation accidents. The operation of nuclear reactors necessarily involves the transportation of radioactive materials from place to place. Fuel must be taken to the reactor site and the wastes from a reactor must be removed to a plant where they can be reprocessed or a place where they can be disposed of. What would happen if there were a traffic accident and radioactivity were released as a result of that accident? Such an accident might happen in a remote, rural area, but it could also happen in an urban, highly populated area, where a great deal of damage could be done.

Several steps have been taken to see that this sort of accident does not happen. First, only a small amount of radioactive material is shipped at one time, so that any accident would discharge only small amounts of radiation. Second, any spent fuel that is removed from a reactor is stored at the reactor plant for at least six months before it can be transported. This reduces the toxicity of the material, since it has been allowed to decay before it is shipped.

But most important, the radioactive materials are shipped in carefully designed and constructed canisters. These canisters are expensive (they cost more than $2 million apiece) and can resist a 48-kmph (30-mph) head-on crash into a solid and unyielding obstacle. They can also withstand envelopment in a gasoline fire for thirty minutes, immersion in water for eight hours, and a puncture test. It should be noted that the temperatures of a gasoline fire would reach about 816° C (1,500° F), far below the 2,760° C (5,000° F) needed to melt the uranium and lead to a meltdown.

Safety experts estimate that if all our energy were derived from nuclear power, there would be one fatality per century due to the release of radioactivity during transportation. There might, of course, be additional deaths due to the accidents themselves (the drivers and crew of the vehicles involved). But since coal power requires at least twice as much transportation than nuclear power, there would likely be far more fatalities due to the use of coal.

Radioactive waste disposal. At present, there is no disposal of the wastes from nuclear power plants in the United States. But by the early 1990s, the accumulated wastes will be placed in specially constructed cylinders, and buried in carefully chosen sites at a depth of about 600 meters (1,970 feet).

The wastes must be kept out of contact with all forms of life for many centuries. When buried deep in the earth, the problem is to keep the material from coming into contact with underground water that might leach through the containers, become contaminated, and eventually rise to the earth's surface, where it would prove harmful to plant and animal life.

For this reason, only earthquake-free sites will be chosen. In addition, only sites that have been free of groundwater for tens of millions of years and where geologists anticipate no water in the future will come under consideration. But even if water should somehow appear, there are safeguards that would prevent radioactive contamination of the earth's surface. First, it would take thousands of years for the water to permeate the rock in which the cylinders are embedded. When the water reached the cylinders, radioactivity would escape very slowly. And, finally, the radioactivity that was leached into water at a depth of 600 meters (1,970 feet) would take at least a thousand years to reach the surface. After all this time, the danger from the wastes would have been dissipated and little harm would be done to surface life. Safety experts estimated that perhaps one fatality a year could be expected from the burial of wastes, if all our electrical energy were derived from nuclear energy.

The advocates of nuclear energy ask us to consider two other aspects of the nuclear waste problem. First, by using up the uranium that is found in the earth, nuclear energy is actually *cleansing* the earth of dangerous radioactivity. Once the surface uranium has been mined and used as fuel and buried as waste, it poses no problem to life.

Second, we are reminded that there are chemical and biological poisons produced by people that are a greater threat to health than any radioactive wastes. For instance, each year the United States imports ten times as much arsenic oxide as we would produce in radioactive waste materials if all our energy were nuclear. A lethal dose of arsenic oxide is only 3 grams (.11 ounces), yet it is not buried to reduce its dangers. Instead, it is used as a herbicide and remains on the earth's surface.

Plutonium. One of the products of the nuclear industry is the element plutonium. Since plutonium can be used as a fuel, it is stored for future use. This presents two problems: (1) plutonium is very toxic and can cause lung cancer if a particle of the substance is inhaled directly into the lungs; and (2) plutonium can be used to make nuclear bombs—a group of terrorists could conceivably steal a supply of plutonium, manufacture a bomb, and use that bomb to threaten a large city.

Nuclear experts tend to discount the seriousness of both problems. Given the safeguards that now exist, they believe that plutonium can be adequately handled and controlled. In the unlikely event that plutonium was allowed to escape from a reactor, it would result in about twenty-five eventual cancer deaths for every pound of plutonium that was released. Thus a full-scale plutonium accident would not result in widespread mortality, but would be limited and relatively small. The experts remind us that more than 45,000 kilograms (10,000 pounds) of plutonium have been spread throughout the world by atomic bomb tests, while about only one-hundredth of a pound would be likely to be released from a full-scale breeder reactor program.

The danger of plutonium theft also decreases in horror if placed in proper perspective. Stealing an adequate supply of plutonium to make a bomb would be a difficult task for a terrorist group. Because plutonium storage sites are well guarded, the terrorists would stand little chance of escaping with their lives.

Furthermore, the construction of the bomb would be an arduous task. Many nuclear experts tell us that the terrorists would find it very expensive, time-consuming, and dangerous. They estimate that it would take at least three people with a great deal of expertise in a variety of technical areas over a period of several months (and at least fifty thousand dollars worth of equipment) to make a bomb from the stolen plutonium. When completed, the bomb would have a 70 percent chance of working, while the people who made it would run a 30 percent chance of being killed for their efforts.

Any bomb produced by a terrorist group, the experts claim, would not cause widespread damage. It would be a "blockbuster" whose explosion would be limited to a relatively confined area. Since terrorists would have easier access to other forms of destruction—such as poisonous gases—it is unlikely that they would resort to the more difficult task of stealing plutonium and building an atomic bomb.

The proponents of nuclear energy rest their case on the relative safety of nuclear power and on its economic advantages. They do not claim nuclear energy is foolproof, merely that it is safer and more attractive than other available sources of energy. The advocates ask us to forget pictures of mushrooming atomic bomb blasts and the many other fears that radioactivity has given rise to. We can, they believe, live comfortably with nuclear energy, without worry and trepidation.

What the proponents want us to do is to accept the reality of a nuclear science and technology that is not perfect, but that has addressed itself to the problems of nuclear energy and answered them. The proponents remind us too that our commitment in time and money to nuclear development has been enormous and that we cannot abandon this commitment overnight without damaging our economy and energy future. It would be unwise, they conclude, for us to turn our backs on nuclear energy in a time of energy crisis. Nuclear energy is here and it is available.

CHAPTER 5
THE CASE AGAINST NUCLEAR ENERGY: ECONOMICS

The opponents of nuclear energy form a diverse group. Many are men and women with little or no scientific background, but with a deep concern for human life and for the harm they claim nuclear power will do to the world. Others are physicists, medical doctors, botanists, or ecologists whose expertise and scientific knowledge have led them to condemn nuclear power and to urge the adoption of some other form of energy. The energy crisis, the opponents argue, can be solved through conservation and through the development of alternative sources of energy such as solar energy, biomass (the use of organic materials to produce energy), wind, or geothermal energy.

One of the strongest arguments that the nuclear critics level against nuclear energy is its expense. Nuclear energy, they claim, has proved to be tremendously expensive and will continue to become more expensive. Since the federal government absorbs much of the costs, the economic burden of nuclear energy has fallen in part on the average taxpayer. If we commit ourselves to a nuclear future, the critics warn, we may have opted for a source of power that will drain our economy and possibly lead to financial disaster.

In order to emphasize the expensiveness of nuclear energy, the opponents have analyzed each step of the reactor

process from the mining of ore to the problem of waste disposal. Their studies show that the nuclear energy program is plagued each step of the way with cost overruns, "hidden costs," vast increases in prices due to inflation, and unforeseen events that raise original cost estimates drastically. These expenses, the critics claim, are only partially recognized by the supporters of nuclear energy, who tend to make nuclear energy sound less costly than it really is.

Fuel. Like oil and natural gas, uranium is now becoming rapidly more expensive and increasingly scarce. In 1973, the price of a pound of uranium oxide was seven dollars. Three years later, this price had risen to forty-two dollars and it continues to rise. In large part, the rise was due to the realization that American uranium resources are limited and that no new substantial finds had been made for some time. This led the nation's chief supplier of nuclear fuel, the Westinghouse Corporation, to default on promises of fuel delivery to its customers. In the future, the critics warn, nuclear reactors may be forced to close down because of a shortage of fuel.

Saunders Miller, a financial analyst and author, estimates that America's known and economically recoverable supplies of uranium could produce 117,000 megawatts (MW) of electricity. Yet reactors now in operation or under construction are designed to generate 120,000 MW—3,000 MW more than the uranium can provide. Moreover, Miller calculates that if additional uranium resources are mined (which are now considered too difficult and expensive to bother with),

At a Westinghouse fuel fabrication plant, fuel rods undergo a final visual inspection. With the aid of number and color coded labels, plant personnel can reconstruct the history of each rod, including the origin of the metals each rod contains.

another 200,000 MW of power could be produced by nuclear reactors. But this number too would fall far short of the anticipated capacity of 510,000 MW which may be needed by the nuclear industry for the year 2000.

Where, the critics ask, is the uranium needed to generate 510,000 MW of power to come from? * The short supply of American uranium will eventually cause uranium prices to soar and will force the nuclear industry to buy fuel from abroad or to extract uranium from shale deposits. If we buy from foreign countries, we will become dependent on them, just as we depend today on oil from the Middle East. Extracting uranium from shale—where the uranium amounts to only a few ounces for every ton of rock—will prove expensive and force the already high price of uranium up even higher.

Fuel Enrichment. Included in the rising costs of fuel will be the costs of enrichment. Before uranium is ready for the reactor, the amount of U-235 in the fuel must be raised so that a chain reaction can be maintained. Fuel enrichment is an expensive process, say the critics, and its costs will rise over the next few years.

At present, only three plants in the United States carry out the enrichment process. In order to provide fuel enrichment for an expanded nuclear program, these plants will have to be expanded and other plants built. The magazine *Business Week* estimates that $30 billion will be needed over the next fifteen years for this program, while Jonathan Kwit-

---

* John Berger, a critic of nuclear energy, estimates that at least 7.3 million metric tons (8 million tons) of uranium will be needed to fuel all the reactors planned for the year 2000, if we are to keep these reactors in operation for the full period of their lifetime (about thirty or forty years). Eight million tons, Berger adds, is more than twice the amount of all the known and estimated reserves in the United States. Berger bases his estimates on plans for nearly a thousand large reactors by the year 2000. These plans have since been abandoned by the nuclear industry. But if Berger's estimates are correct, uranium to fuel even the three hundred fifty plants now planned may be in short supply.

ney of the *Wall Street Journal* believes the costs of enrichment plants will be closer to $60 billion. Whatever the final costs, however, fuel enrichment will add to the expenses of an already expensive nuclear industry.

The Costs of the Reactor Plant. The costs of building a reactor are already higher than for building a coal-burning plant of comparable generating capacity and are still rising. In 1967, the Atomic Energy Commission (AEC) estimated that a reactor would cost $134 per kilowatt hour (kwh) of generating capacity. In reality, the critics claim, costs were much higher and amounted to about $200 to $400 per kwh. By 1976, these expenses had risen to $645 and by 1979 they were nearly $1,000.

Moreover, reactor plant construction is constantly plagued by vast cost overruns. A reactor built by Boston Edison Company on Cape Cod Bay and completed in 1972 cost four times more at completion than its original estimates had allowed. In 1976, a study by the Massachusetts Institute of Technology showed that the average cost overrun for reactor construction was 100 percent, or twice the original estimate. With this kind of record, the critics ask, how can we regard nuclear energy as an economically desirable source?

But the costs of building a reactor are only a part of the total costs involved in the reactor's life. The reactor must be maintained for its lifetime of thirty to forty years. This requires constant surveillance for malfunctions and safety hazards. And it must be "decommissioned" at the end of its lifetime. Decommissioning means that the reactor must be rendered safe—over its lifetime, it will have become contaminated with radiation—and harmless.

Reactor maintenance, the critics point out, has proved to be a particularly expensive project. Reactors must be routinely shut down for a few weeks each year to check for leakages or any other problems that may have arisen. During these shutdowns, the plant produces no power and electricity must be generated by another source. If routine inspections uncover malfunctions, then additional time must be taken for repairs and improvements.

Routine shutdowns, however, are not the only stoppages a reactor may experience. Many reactors are forced to stop the generation of electricity because of equipment failures. Others may be required to slow down the plant's activity because of environmental reasons. As a result, very few reactors in the United States work to their full capacity and produce the amount of power they were designed to produce. A study by the Council of Economic Priorities, an antinuclear group, concluded that the average reactor functioned only 40 percent of the time.

The opponents of nuclear energy argue that this is a poor record for plants that have been so expensive to build. But the opponents are more concerned with the higher utility bills that result from the poor performance of reactors than with the poor performance itself. In order to provide energy for its customers when a nuclear plant is closed down, a utility company buys electricity from other companies. This electricity is bought at a higher rate than is usually paid for electricity and the extra costs are passed on to the consumers, who end up paying higher electric bills for every day that a nuclear plant is shut down.

Shutdowns may occur for any number of reasons. In 1972 and 1973, The New England Electric Company took six months to replace bolts in one of its reactors. The discovery of cracks in the emergency cooling system at a plant in Illinois led to a ruling by the Nuclear Regulatory Commission (NRC) that closed down almost half the reactors in the country for inspection. Similarly, the incident at Three Mile Island in 1979 led to the shutdown of other reactors that had been constructed by the same company until their safety could be assured.

Studies by the Council of Economic Priorities and by David Comey, an antinuclear activist, have shown that reactor stoppages may increase in number in the future. These studies claim that large reactors are less reliable than smaller ones. Since the nuclear industry is now oriented toward the construction of large reactors of the 1000 MW range, this means that reactor efficiency may decline. Furthermore, the same studies indicate that large reactors age poorly and will be more prone to break down during their later years due to corrosion, metal fatigue, and radiation buildup.

The Costs of Reprocessing. Nuclear energy experts estimate that by 1990 at least four reprocessing plants will be needed for the two hundred reactors planned for that time. These reprocessing plants will cost about a billion dollars each and will take the spent fuel from operating reactors, separating what can be used again from what must be disposed of as waste. The chief problems with reprocessing, the critics say, is that it has not yet worked commercially and will probably cost far more than is now estimated, once the plants have been put into commission.

The three attempts at the construction of reprocessing plants to date do not give nuclear proponents much cause for optimism. America's first reprocessing plant opened in West Valley, New York, in 1966, and was operated by Nuclear Fuel Services (NFS), a private concern. The plant was poorly designed and had trouble from the very beginning. It lost more than a million dollars a year, in spite of subsidies from the federal government and the state of New York. Finally, dozens of workers at the plant were contaminated with radioactivity and West Valley was closed down for extensive repairs. NFS abandoned the plant entirely when it learned that $600 million were needed to reopen the plant safely— a sum more than twenty times the plant's original costs.

A second and third attempt at the construction of safe and reliable reprocessing plants were made at Morris, Illinois, and Barnwell, South Carolina. The Morris plant was completed in 1974 by General Electric at a cost of $64 million. For a number of reasons, the plant proved to be inoperable and General Electric chose to close it down rather than spend the $100 million that experts estimated was needed for improvements. The plant at Barnwell, on the other hand, had cost Allied General Nuclear Services $250 million by 1976, but still could not meet safety standards set by the federal government. The *Wall Street Journal* called the plant "one of the biggest white elephants of the nuclear age."

The Costs of Nuclear Waste Disposal. No one knows what reprocessing plants will cost, the critics argue, because no successful plant has been built. Similarly, no one knows what the expenses of waste disposal will be, since no waste disposal program has yet been devised. In the words of a report issued by the Environmental Protection Agency (EPA), "even assuming the technical capability exists to insure total containment for the hazardous lifetime of nuclear wastes, the cost of implementing the means to contain these wastes is enormous."

These costs would include the construction of containers strong enough to hold the wastes safely, the solidification of wastes now in liquid form, shipment to a disposal sight, and final disposal (probably by burial). A study by the Energy Research and Development Administration (ERDA) estimates that disposal of 1.9 million liters (500,000 gallons) of high-level wastes now stored beneath the closed reprocessing plant in West Valley could cost over $500 million. NFS, the company that ran the plant, has left only $2.5 million in a perpetual fund to pay for disposal once an acceptable method has been worked out. The critics warn that any method for waste disposal is likely to prove far more expensive than anyone now assumes.

The Costs of Breeder Reactors. Nuclear opponents see the development of breeder reactors as the most expensive part of the nuclear power program. Breeders were once scheduled to go into operation by the 1980s, but have been shelved until the 1990s. Meanwhile, the costs for breeder research and development are rising rapidly. Originally, a breeder reactor was to cost about 10 percent more than a conventional reactor. But experts now estimate that a breeder will more than likely be as much as 275 percent more expensive than other reactors.

These estimates are borne out by experience. The Clinch River demonstration breeder, in Tennessee, originally planned at a cost of $700 million, has now cost the federal government $1.8 billion—and may cost $2 billion before it is completed. Whatever its final cost, it is a comparatively small reactor—350 to 400 MW—and will be used primarily to study breeder reactor performance. A second breeder in Richland, Washington, was planned at a cost of $87 million, but has actually cost $750 million.

If these two reactors offer any indication, the critics say, breeder technology will be very expensive. By the time one hundred breeders are built, the government will have spent at least $200 billion on breeder research and development alone. This overwhelming commitment is unwarranted, the critics conclude, because breeders have not yet proved to be commercially viable. Nor is it certain that the public will accept breeders, since they offer greater hazards than do conventional reactors.

The Costs of Insurance. One of the hidden costs mentioned by nuclear opponents that will add to the expense of nuclear energy is insurance. At this time, no private insurance company offers adequate coverage for a nuclear reactor accident. Insurance companies fear that such an accident might be too expensive and too widespread for them to handle. The federal government, through the Price-Anderson Bill, now offers $560 million to cover accidents that may occur.

This $560 million is intended to cover all damage that is done. But according to a Nuclear Regulatory Commission study made in 1975, an accident could result in $14 billion worth of damage. Under the Price-Anderson Bill, the government would pay out $560 million in damage claims, but would bear no responsibility for the other $13.4 billion. As a Columbia University study has put it: "The decision to limit liability represents a determination that a major share of the costs of an accident should be borne by its victims." In other words, the costs of an accident would fall largely on the people who had suffered most from it.

The Dangers of a Nuclear Monopoly. The American government frowns on monopolies and for more than seventy years has worked to break them up wherever they occur. Yet if we commit ourselves to a nuclear future, the critics claim, we are committing ourselves to a monopoly by the nuclear industry. Because of the overwhelming costs of nuclear power, a total commitment to nuclear energy would exclude the development of other alternative forms of energy. The American economy, strained by inflation and the falling value of the dollar, cannot support the nuclear industry and, at the same time, pay for solar research or for research into other energy fields.

In 1975, the federal budget provided $200,000 for research into solar energy. In the same year, more than $1 billion (more than five hundred times as much) was slated for the nuclear industry. President Carter's most recent energy program provides more money for solar research, but if we choose to expand the nuclear program, the discrepancy between the funds provided for solar energy and the funds provided for nuclear energy will grow ever wider. It is now time, the critics say, to choose between a future monopolized by the nuclear industry and one where a variety of energy sources are developed.

Nuclear opponents also recognize a second problem that will arise from a nuclear monopoly. Conventional reactors and breeder reactors generate only one form of energy that can be used by the consumer: electricity. A nuclear future would be an electric future. As fossil fuels such as oil and natural gas began to disappear, we would become increasingly dependent upon electricity to satisfy all our energy needs, from plowing fields and harvesting grain to the heating of homes, and from transportation to the running of factories.

In order to cope with an all electrical future, the present economy would have to be overhauled. Buses and trains would have to be electrified. Factories would have to be established to manufacture synthetic fuels for airplanes and other machines that still required liquid fuels. Everywhere, industries that use coal or oil would have to be converted to electrical power. The costs of this transition, the critics warn, would be enormous and would place a severe strain on economic life.

Two other factors should also be taken into consideration. An all nuclear future would concentrate a great deal of power into the hands of a few corporations that controlled the nuclear industry. And it would also increase the power of the federal government. Already, there have been widespread complaints about the power of oil companies and utilities to raise prices at will, control the amount of energy available to the public, and affect the national economy. An all nuclear future, the critics claim, would enhance that power and make us all the pawns of corporate decisions.

A nuclear future, too, would lead to the broadening of government powers, in order to deal with the possibility of theft of radioactive materials. Stolen plutonium could be made into a bomb that could be used to threaten a large city. Extraordinary measures such as martial law might be required to recover the stolen material. As Russell W. Myers, a lawyer, has written, "once a quantity of plutonium had been stolen, the case for literally turning the country upside down to get it back would be overwhelming."

Already, a "federal nuclear police force" has been suggested as a means to combat the work of nuclear terrorists. But even if such a force is never established, surveillance of nuclear installations would have to increase. Guards would have to be stationed at reactor plants. Nuclear experts estimate that a hundred-member security force will be needed at every nuclear site, from reactors to reprocessing plants. These security forces will add unknown costs to nuclear energy, the critics claim.

In conclusion, the opponents of nuclear energy find nuclear power to be highly uneconomical and therefore an undesirable form of energy. The enormous costs of reactor construction, unreliable plants that generate only part of the energy they were designed to produce, and the rising price and increasing scarcity of uranium are only part of the picture. The unknown costs of fuel reprocessing and waste disposal, as well as many hidden costs, must also be taken into consideration. When all these factors are added together, the critics argue that nuclear energy can only be seen as a very expensive road for our nation to follow. Do we want, they ask, to attach ourselves to a program that may not work and that will leave us stranded, years from now, without adequate energy and with an economy that has been strained to the breaking point?

The opponents of nuclear energy must not be seen as pessimists with no program of their own. Most nuclear critics envision a future where a variety of energy sources have replaced the depleted resources of oil and natural gas. Many of these alternative sources have already been mentioned, but the one most frequently advocated by nuclear critics is solar energy. They admit that solar energy may prove expensive to develop, but claim that in the final analysis it will never be as expensive as nuclear energy. The problem is to divert the funds now committed to nuclear energy to solar research and development. If that is done, the critics say, solar energy can become in a short time a reliable and economical source of power.

CHAPTER 6
THE CASE AGAINST NUCLEAR ENERGY: SAFETY

The high costs of nuclear energy can be traced in large part to one cause: the effort to make nuclear plants as safe as possible. Federal regulations require that every reactor pass stiff tests before it can be licensed to operate. Only materials of high quality and manufactured with the greatest care can be used in the construction of the plant. Every part and section of the completed reactor must be judged safe and sound and free of flaws that could lead to accidents.

In order to meet these difficult requirements, the nuclear industry has spent enormous sums of money to make reactors safe, reliable, and accident-free. Original price estimates are constantly revised and raised to pay for construction alterations that decrease the chances of malfunction. As a result, nuclear proponents now claim that nuclear plants generate electricity more safely than any other kind of plant. The nuclear critics, however, disagree completely with this judgment.

For the critics, there are two problems—mechanical failure and human failure—that can never be overcome no matter how "perfect" reactor systems are made. Everything man-made is subject to error. Cars break down; toasters come with defective parts. Even highly sophisticated programs like the Apollo moon project fall prey to mechanical malfunctions and related problems. How then, the nuclear opponents ask, can a reactor be judged harmless, when it too can break down?

The same can be said of the human element, necessary in the functioning of every reactor. Experts in every field sometimes make mistakes or are remiss in their responsibilities. Sickness, a momentary flash of anger, or fatigue may cause lapses in judgment or ability. Who is to say that the technicians that operate our large reactors will remain at all times consistently levelheaded and rational?

Human error and mechanical failure do not present much of a problem in ordinary circumstances. The breakdown of a car or an accident at a coal-burning power plant rarely causes much harm or damage. In the case of a nuclear reactor, however, a similar malfunction could prove disastrous. Radioactivity could be released into the atmosphere and render whole areas uninhabitable, the critics warn. Many people—possibly thousands—would die from acute radiation poisoning, from cancers that would develop many years later, and from genetic defects. For this reason, the opponents conclude, nuclear energy carries too great a risk to life and health to be considered a viable source of energy. In its place, we must seek and develop other forms of energy, where mechanical failure or human error will prove less harmful and dangerous.

NUCLEAR ACCIDENTS
CAN HAPPEN

Nuclear opponents reject the findings of the Rasmussen Report, the study mentioned in chapter 4 which claimed that the worst possible reactor accident could happen only once in a million years. The same report also argued that a meltdown, which might happen once in fifty years, would result in ten immediate deaths, five hundred eventual deaths from cancer, and cause $300 million in damage to property.

These figures, the critics claim, are wrong on every point. Reactor accidents will occur far more frequently than he estimates and they will be far more destructive than he concludes. Amory Lovins, a noted physicist, has studied the Rasmussen Report closely. Its "data and methodology," he writes, "yield absurd results when used to predict the likelihood of major multiple failures which have actually occurred." When Lovins applied Rasmussen's technique to one possible sequence of failures in boiling-water reactors, he found that the failures should occur only once in many billions of reactor-years. "Yet," he pointed out, "at least fifteen such accidents have already occurred in the USA." If the Rasmussen Report could be so wrong in this instance, the critics ask, what assurance do we have that its findings are at all accurate?

Other studies also conflict with Rasmussen's findings. The United States Environmental Protection Agency claims that his figures are ten times too low and that a reactor accident could result in ten times the number of deaths and ten times the amount of destruction that Rasmussen allows for. The Union of Concerned Scientists, a group critical of nuclear power, finds Rasmussen's figures sixteen times short of what would really happen in a nuclear accident.

In addition to these failures, nuclear opponents also accuse Rasmussen of ignoring reactor problems that would have raised his figures. Rasmussen, for instance, did not consider the possibility of plant sabotage or the theft of plutonium by terrorist groups. Nor did his report evaluate the problems of fuel reprocessing or the handling of nuclear wastes. And, finally, it did not take into consideration the hazards involved in a breeder reactor program, even though the Atomic Energy Commission estimates that the United States will have many breeders operating within the next twenty-five years. With all these omissions, the critics ask, how can Rasmussen be taken seriously? *

* The critics also argue that the objectivity of the Rasmussen Report must be called into question. Much of the report was done at the headquarters of the Atomic Energy Commission and by strongly pronuclear scientists and engineers. In addition, parts of the report were subcontracted to private firms such as Boeing and Aeroject Nuclear, which have substantial interests in expanding the nuclear industry.

There are other scientific and highly regarded studies, the opponents claim, that give a far more accurate picture of what will happen in a reactor accident than the Rasmussen Report gives. The first is the Brookhaven Report, issued by the Atomic Energy Commission in 1957. The reactors studied by the Brookhaven Report were small—between 100 and 200 megawatts (MW), because no large, 1,000-MW, reactors had yet been constructed.

The report imagined an accident in a plant approximately thirty miles from a large city. During the accident, 50 percent of the reactor core's radioactivity is released into the atmosphere. This would result in 3,400 immediate deaths and $7 billion in damage (in 1957 dollars; today this would be at least $20 billion). No estimate was made of eventual cancer deaths. Another study released in 1957, this time by the Engineering Research Institute of the University of Michigan, raised these casualty figures even higher. This report concluded that 133,000 people would die "under maximum radioactive release conditions" and that 181,000 would be injured.

In 1964 and 1965, the Atomic Energy Commission once again looked into the nature of a reactor accident. The result was a study that was not released by the commission (the critics say it was suppressed) until 1973, when a coalition of environmentalist groups threatened to sue for its release under the U.S. Freedom of Information Act. In this report, the AEC foresaw 45,000 dying as the result of a "worst possible accident." An additional 100,000 would be injured and there would be $17 billion in damage (in 1965 dollars; $34 billion in 1979 dollars). The accident would contaminate an area the size of Pennsylvania for five hundred years and release, among other radioactive materials, two highly toxic isotopes, strontium 90 and cesium 137.

The critics admit that these studies—the Brookhaven Report, the investigation by the research institute at the University of Michigan, and the AEC report of 1965—have their inadequacies, just like the Rasmussen Report. No one can really know what will happen in an accident until one takes place. But these reports do tend to show that a reactor accident is likely to take place and that it would probably be more damaging than nuclear proponents are willing to admit. With findings like these, the critics ask, how can anyone be confident in a nuclear future?

NUCLEAR ACCIDENTS
HAVE HAPPENED

How could a nuclear accident occur? According to the nuclear opponents, a flaw or malfunction could appear at almost any point in the operation of a reactor. The safety systems established by nuclear technicians and engineers are simply not able to provide proper security. In the words of the Union of Concerned Scientists: "It is not simply that one or two vital links are demonstrably weak. It is that the whole structure is unsound." In addition, the union claims that reactor safety systems and procedures are based on engineering "whose quality and scope are broadly and seriously deficient."

To emphasize their belief in the inadequacy of reactors, the critics cite examples where human or mechanical error resulted in an accident or a near accident.

■ In 1971, tests at the AEC's Oak Ridge laboratories showed that fuel rods commonly used in reactors would buckle, swell, and rupture at temperatures far lower than they would have to withstand during a loss-of-coolant accident. The tests, however, were discontinued, even though they had revealed dangerous problems in the design of the rods.

■ The Zion Station nuclear plant near Chicago opened in 1973. The next year it had to be closed because its emergency core cooling system was found to have been incorrectly wired and would not have worked in case of an accident.

■ In September 1974, the AEC closed down twenty-one of the fifty nuclear plants working in the country at that time to check for leaks in pipes. Leaks were discovered in two reactors and cracks were found in a third.

■ In February 1975, steam generator piping ruptured at Wisconsin Electric's plant at Point Beach on Lake Michigan. Previously, the AEC had declared that this type of accident was so unlikely that the chances it would occur could be discounted.

■ In March 1975, a technician was making a routine search for an air leak in the cable room of the two reactors at Brown's Ferry, Alabama. The cable room, which was located just below the general control room shared by both reactors, contained cables leading to unit 1 and to unit 2. These cables controlled the flow of electricity to the routine and emergency core cooling systems of the two reactors, so that any damage to the cable room would prove hazardous to the security of the plant.

The technician and an assistant used a lighted candle (this was standard plant procedure) to test for air leaks near a spot that had been stuffed with flammable polyurethane foam. Suddenly, the flame from the candle was sucked into a hole and the foam was ignited. The men attempted to put out the fire with a chemical fire extinguisher, but failed. Fifteen minutes later, they warned a guard about the fire and a few minutes after that an alarm was sounded.

The fire, which eventually destroyed sixteen hundred cables, led quickly to a number of malfunctions. First, the instrument panels in the control room began to react abnormally and chaotically. A plant operator managed to reinsert the control rods into the reactor core. This brought the chain reaction to a halt, but did not prevent the possibility of a meltdown, since the fuel in the core continued to heat.

At this time, it was discovered that the reactor's normal cooling system and its emergency cooling system were not working properly. The instruments that relayed reactor temperatures and pressures to the control room were likewise dead, leaving the technicians with no clear idea of what was taking place. As the plant operators worked to bring the crisis under control, smoke and fumes began to fill the control room because of the failure of the plant's fire-fighting system.

The accident at Brown's Ferry, however, did not lead to a meltdown and a normal shutdown was achieved within fourteen hours. But it did underline what the critics have said about plant malfunctions and human error. In a few short minutes, a fire had disabled a large nuclear plant. Disaster had been averted in this case, but could it be prevented in accidents in the future?

■ For nuclear critics, the most remarkable example of reactor shortcomings and scientific bungling is the accident at Three Mile Island in March 1979, mentioned earlier. When the first investigations of the accident were published, they showed that the accident had resulted from a long series of errors. Furthermore, it was also found that disaster had been prevented by a chance action of a technician and not by a carefully followed program set up to deal with accidents.

The first failure at Three Mile Island involved negligence. Three feedwater pumps had been taken out of commission against federal regulations. Only one pump was working the day of the accident and it left no margin of safety when the accident occurred. Second, a relief valve in the primary coolant loop opened, as it was supposed to do, to let overheated water escape. But then it failed to close, causing a dangerous drop in pressure.

At this time, at least one water-level indicator in the control room seems to have given a wrong reading. This caused a technician to assume the situation had been brought under control, when it had not. For some reason, which no one understands, control room technicians then turned off the emergency and the primary cooling pumps. One expert has described this act as "sheer folly." Finally, when the reactor core overheated, it created an *unexpected* problem—a

**No steam has risen from these cooling towers since the
Three Mile Island Nuclear Power plant, near Harrisburg, Pa.,
was shut down due to radiation leakage in March of 1979.**

dangerous, explosive bubble of hydrogen gas. For this, the experts were unprepared. Although the bubble was later shown to be less dangerous than was first thought, the appearance of a new and unanticipated malfunction caused the critics to wonder if other similar problems could arise in the future.

Over the past ten years, the critics claim, reactors have proved time and again to have serious flaws. Yet still we continue to plan for a nuclear future and to anticipate the construction of hundreds of new reactors. Will a full-scale accident have to occur, they ask, before we see the folly of nuclear energy and before we realize that the risks of a nuclear future far outweigh its rewards?

THE DANGERS OF RADIATION

The chief danger presented by nuclear energy is radiation. The alpha particles, beta particles, and gamma rays emitted by radioactive materials can penetrate the cells of living creatures and cause great damage. Acute radiation sickness often leads to death in a matter of days. But radioactivity can also cause long-term damage that eventually appears as some form of cancer, perhaps twenty or thirty years after exposure. When radiation penetrates reproductive cells, it increases the chances of birth defects in future generations of children.

The trouble with radiation is that no one knows how much is harmful. A dose that kills one person may do little injury to another. The federal government has set standards of exposure that many scientists believe are safe and adequate, as long as no one exceeds the legal dosage. Nuclear critics disagree. They believe that there is already enough radiation in the atmosphere—from bomb tests, from medical and dental equipment, and from natural radiation—and that the release of even more radiation from a large number of reactors could prove exceedingly dangerous.

The critics point to evidence that shows a clear relationship between cancer and all levels of radiation exposure, including tiny doses. Dr. John Gofman, a medical doctor who also has a Ph.D. in nuclear physical chemistry, and Dr. Arthur Tamplin, a former employee of the AEC, have conducted studies that lead them to conclude that there can be no safe dose of radioactivity. They argue that if the American public were exposed to the amounts of radiation allowed by law, thirty-two thousand eventual cancer deaths would result, plus a large number of genetically induced deaths. This means that all workers in nuclear plants run a higher than normal chance of death by cancer and that all releases of radiation from reactors should be considered dangerous.

In another study, Dr. Ernest Sternglass, a physics professor at the University of Pittsburgh, found another correlation between radiation and cancer. Dr. Sternglass estimated that 400,000 infant and prenatal deaths had resulted from the bomb tests in Nevada during the 1950s. Dr. Gofman and Dr. Tamplin looked at Sternglass's work and found his estimates too high, but they concluded, nevertheless, that at least 4,000 deaths could be attributed to the Nevada tests.

Radiation is routinely leaked from reactors, but most experts believe that these routine emissions are harmless. The greatest amount of radioactive release, of course, would come from a major accident. But it can also come, the critics claim, from other stages of the nuclear program, from mining through waste disposal.

For instance, Robert Pohl, a physicist at Cornell University, has pointed out that there are dangerous amounts of thorium 230 in uranium tailings. Tailings are the refuse material thrown away during the mining of ore. One hundred million tons of uranium tailings already exist in the western states. By the year 2000, if the nuclear industry continues to expand as planned, these tailings will amount to twenty billion tons which will contain significant traces of thorium 230, as well as other toxic substances such as radon 222 and polonium 233.

The radioactive half-life of thorium 230 is 80,000 years. This means that a ton of thorium 230 would take 80,000 years to lose half of its radioactivity. Since it takes about ten half-lives to render a radioactive substance relatively harmless, it would be 800,000 years before the thorium 230 would no longer pose a threat to life. In the meanwhile, Dr. Pohl estimates that the thorium will cause an average of more than a thousand deaths a year from cancer. These annual effects will gradually increase until more than eleven million people have died.

One of the most dangerous materials handled by the nuclear industry is plutonium. Dr. John Gofman, who was mentioned earlier, has concentrated much of his scientific research on the problems raised by plutonium toxicity. He concludes that if the nuclear industry lost only one part in every ten thousand parts of plutonium it will manufacture in the future, then an average of 500,000 annual deaths from lung cancer could eventually be expected. Over fifty years, he adds, this would amount to 25 million deaths.

Even if Dr. Gofman's figures prove to be wrong, critics maintain that the handling of plutonium by the nuclear industry leaves little room for optimism. Robert Gillette, in an article that appeared in *Science* (September 20 and 27, 1974), accused the industry of gross neglect and irresponsibility when it came to plutonium. The record shows, he wrote, a "dismal repetition" of plutonium leaks, of employees who fail to follow established procedure, of violations of federal regulations, and of plutonium spills in plant corridors and in some cases beyond plant boundaries into cars, homes, a restaurant, and a sheriff's office in New York. If this is the history of handling plutonium, the critics ask, how can the nuclear industry be trusted to handle the toxic element in the future, when larger amounts of it will be produced?

BREEDERS, REPROCESSING PLANTS, AND WASTE DISPOSAL: THE GREAT UNKNOWNS

The chances for radioactive contamination increase, the nuclear opponents tell us, when we consider the side of the nuclear industry that has not yet been developed: breeder reactors, reprocessing plants, and the disposal of radioactive wastes. Perhaps the greatest danger, they conclude, will come from the breeder program.

The core of a breeder reactor will contain 0.9 to 3.6 metric tons (2 to 4 tons) of plutonium. This makes the core of a breeder reactor potentially far more dangerous than the core of a conventional reactor. An accident that led to a meltdown in a breeder could cause the plutonium fuel to reach a "critical mass" that might result in a nuclear explosion. Such an explosion would release far more radioactivity into the atmosphere than an explosion at a conventional reactor would release.

According to the critics, breeders are susceptible to two malfunctions that could lead to a meltdown. First, the breeders now under development use liquid sodium as a coolant. But sodium is an element that will explode if it comes into contact with water, which it could do if the reactor developed a leak. The second problem in the breeder is the fuel rods, which must be able to withstand conditions within the breeder core without swelling and breaking.

Two cases of breeder malfunction in the past give the critics little hope that breeder technology will work. The Fermi reactor, located near Detroit, was working at one-tenth its power when an accident occurred, followed by a meltdown. Experts who looked into the meltdown later concluded that a nuclear explosion had been narrowly averted. The second incident took place in the Soviet Union, a country that intends to expand its nuclear program rapidly during the next few years. A Soviet breeder had to be shut down after water reached the sodium coolant, resulting in a meltdown.

Finally, the critics argue, the plutonium in a breeder offers an ideal source of bomb material for a terrorist group. Moreover, the critics contend that it would not be overwhelmingly difficult for a terrorist group to construct a bomb. With the right sort of expertise and determination, they could build a device that could level the World Trade Center in New York or some other familiar landmark. Indeed,

Ted Turner, a physicist who has designed several nuclear bombs for the American government, expects that it is only a matter of time before terrorists do explode their first nuclear bomb.

Reprocessing plants and waste disposal programs are other areas where faulty technology and poor planning have resulted in radiation leakages, the critics claim. The reprocessing plant at West Valley, New York, was closed after it released radioactive materials and contaminated several workers. In short, the critics say, nuclear technology has yet to prove that it can make reprocessing safe and reliable, but plans are nevertheless going forward to expand the nuclear industry.

Attempts at storage and disposal of wastes have likewise led to problems. Seventy-five percent of America's nuclear defense wastes are stored at the Hanford Reservation in the state of Washington. But since storage began at Hanford, more than 1.9 million liters (500,000 gallons) of radioactive materials have leaked from their containers. An AEC report blamed part of the leakage on worn-out containers and an inadequate monitoring system, but found that the Atlantic Richfield Company, which was responsible for the material, had been negligent.

At present, there is no program for radioactive waste disposal. In the 1950s and 1960s, low level nuclear wastes were placed in containers and dumped into the Atlantic Ocean off the coasts of Maryland and Delaware. These containers have already begun to leak, due to the effects of salt water and corrosion, and the practice was halted in 1970. Any waste disposal plan adopted in the future, the critics warn, will have to make certain that the wastes will be secure for hundreds of thousands of years.

The critics remind us that machines can malfunction and that humans can be negligent or make wrong decisions that can lead to disaster. They claim that nuclear accidents are more likely to occur than nuclear proponents have estimated and that radiation is far more dangerous than the nuclear industry would have us believe. The critics believe that the elaborate safety programs that have been developed to avoid nuclear catastrophe are inadequate and that the public should not be led into thinking that nuclear energy is a safe and reasonable source of energy.

With all the problems that are involved in the production of nuclear energy, the critics ask us to assess the risks of a nuclear future. Do we want a technology that has proved to be faulty in the past to develop into the huge industry that is planned? The answer, they claim, can only be no.

CHAPTER 7
THE POLITICS OF NUCLEAR ENERGY

Public interest in nuclear energy has made it one of the important political issues of our time. At stake are questions that will affect not only this generation, but also generations to come. The choice is difficult and formidable. If we reject a nuclear future, nuclear proponents tell us, we are condemning ourselves to energy shortages, a slowdown in economic development, and a lower standard of living. If we accept nuclear power, the critics promise us a future threatened by the chance of reactor accidents and the spread of radioactivity. Clearly, these are questions that must be carefully weighed and considered.

In large part, public opinion will determine the outcome of the nuclear energy controversy. Already, antinuclear activists have been successful in slowing down and, in several cases, stopping the construction of new reactors. On the other side, the nuclear industry each year spends large sums of money on campaigns designed to convince the public that nuclear energy is safe and desirable. The battle for the hearts and minds of American voters is likely to become more intense in the future as the energy crisis increases and as new reactors are built.

THE CAMPAIGN FOR
NUCLEAR ENERGY

During the 1950s and 1960s, the proponents of nuclear energy acquired a tremendous lead over the critics. After 1953, government and private industry combined their efforts to develop the nuclear industry. Businessmen, senators, industrialists, and Washington bureaucrats joined in a belief that nuclear energy would provide a cheap and pollution-free source of power for centuries to come. The government liberally granted funds to universities and private firms for nuclear research and development. In return, industry, sometimes reluctantly, accepted government regulation.

The relationship that developed between government and private industry in the early days of nuclear energy, however, was more partnership than opposition. No one in government took a stand against nuclear power and regulation amounted to little more than close scrutiny of government grants to see that money was spent wisely and insistence on the development of safe reactors. The comfortable relationship led to the rapid development of nuclear energy, as it also led to the belief, still predominant in government and industrial circles today, that America must commit itself to a nuclear future. Until recently, most of the people of the United States have shared this belief.

Government regulation of nuclear energy during peacetime dates from 1946, when the Congress established its eighteen-member Joint Committee on Atomic Energy and created the federal Atomic Energy Commission. From the beginning, both groups proved to be strongly pronuclear. The Joint Committee, with members from both the House of Representatives and the Senate, regularly voted funding for nuclear projects. Two congressmen, Chet Holifield (a Democrat from California) and Craig Hosmer (a Republican from California) who sat on the committee were among the chief advocates of nuclear energy in Congress and urged their colleagues to support the expansion of the industry.

The Atomic Energy Commission, a division of the executive branch of government under the control of the president, encouraged the nuclear industry through grants and subsidies and through the use of pronuclear propaganda and information. It controlled a large part of the money provided by the Congress for nuclear research and decided which projects should be funded. The AEC published numerous pamphlets and other educational aids—often written and produced for the average person who knew little about science—that supported the nuclear program and emphasized the advantages of nuclear energy. These programs often reached large audiences. In 1972, for instance, the AEC had 120 films in circulation which were viewed by an estimated 3.5 million people, not including a much wider audience that was reached when they were shown on television. In 1974, the AEC was replaced by the Energy Research and Development Administration (ERDA) and the Nuclear Regulatory Commission (NRC).

Efforts by the federal government to establish a favorable climate of opinion for nuclear energy have been joined by efforts from private industry. Several research groups, including the Atomic Industrial Forum, the Electric Power Research Institute, Reddy Kilowatt, and others, are funded by corporations interested in the development of nuclear industry. These groups play an important part in bringing information to the public and in dispelling fears about nuclear problems.

■ The Atomic Industrial Forum (AIF). The AIF is perhaps the most influential pronuclear group. Located in New York, it provides a rich supply of nuclear information for interested persons who may wish to rebut the critics of nuclear energy. This information reaches federal lawmakers, state legislators, and others involved in nuclear issues. *Press INFO*, the monthly newsletter of the AIF, is sent to numerous editors and reporters who write on nuclear problems. Each year, the AIF offers an award "for public understanding of nuclear energy by the news media."

These efforts have made the Atomic Industrial Forum the

most aggressive of the pronuclear organizations. Well funded and efficiently managed, it seeks to confront criticism of nuclear energy wherever it may appear. The opponents of nuclear energy have accused the AIF of distortions and outright lies. Proponents, however, have welcomed its work and regard the AIF as one of the most important defenders of the pronuclear movement.

■ The Electric Power Research Institute (EPRI). EPRI has stated that one of its most important goals is to "strengthen the nuclear power option and resolve nuclear safety issues." It is an organization of several utility companies with offices in Palo Alto, California, and Washington, D.C. EPRI carries out research projects in the energy field, often in cooperation with government agencies such as ERDA and the Department of the Interior.

■ Federation of Americans Supporting Science and Technology (FASST). Funded by several utility companies, FASST has established Energy Youth Councils at colleges and universities and sends nuclear information to more than one thousand campus newspapers. Its aim is to defuse fears concerning the nuclear industry and to gain young nuclear advocates.

■ Reddy Kilowatt. Reddy Kilowatt of Connecticut is one of the most prolific producers of pronuclear literature and information. Reddy Kilowatt has also provided seminars to utility executives in order to instruct them on how to handle the more vocal opponents of nuclear energy.

■ The American Nuclear Energy Council (ANEC). ANEC is a pronuclear lobbying center for nuclear manufacturers and related industries. Located in Washington, D.C., it labors to maintain a pronuclear climate of opinion among the nation's lawmakers and among those who staff the government's nuclear agencies.

■ The American Nuclear Society (ANS). The ANS is an association of some ten thousand scientists, engineers, and administrators of nuclear plants. It is centered in Hinesdale, Illinois, and maintains a speaker's bureau to provide pronuclear speakers for interested groups. The ANS also makes an effort to coordinate the work of nuclear advocates throughout the country so that the best possible case can be made for nuclear energy.

THE CAMPAIGN AGAINST NUCLEAR ENERGY

To confront the well-entrenched supporters of nuclear energy in government, private industry, and academic quarters, the antinuclear movement has acted on a number of fronts. In most cases, these efforts have involved the use of law, government regulatory agencies, or state commissions to bring a halt to nuclear projects because of potential damage to the environment or because of unreasonable costs related to plant construction. In a few instances, the critics have resorted to more dramatic means to make their case known—to demonstrations and sit-ins at nuclear installations—that sometimes end in arrest.

Antinuclear groups tend to be smaller and much less wealthy than pronuclear groups. They include numerous local groups such as the Clamshell Alliance of New England, the Sierra Club of California, and the Palmetto League of South Carolina, some of which have become nationally famous for their environmental work. They also include organizations like Ralph Nader's Critical Mass and the Union of Concerned Scientists, both of which have been highly effective in disseminating antinuclear information.

Located in Washington, D.C., Critical Mass is the antinuclear arm of Ralph Nader's "consumer crusade." It brings antinuclear activists and concerned citizens from across the nation together to coordinate antinuclear activity and discuss strategy. It regularly lobbies Congress on the dangers and problems involved in nuclear energy. Critical Mass promises in the future to be as much a headache for the nuclear industry as Nader's earlier attacks on the automobile companies were for that industry.

But perhaps the most prestigious group of nuclear critics, from a scientific point of view, is the Union of Concerned Scientists (UCS) of Cambridge, Massachusetts. As its name suggests, UCS is made up of men and women from a variety of scientific fields. UCS has carried on a long battle with the Atomic Energy Commission over the dangers of reactor emergency cooling systems. It has delivered a statement to the White House, signed by twenty-three hundred scientists who have grave doubts about the safety of nuclear energy. Many members of the UCS have published papers dealing with nuclear problems.

The antinuclear groups mentioned here and others have successfully used federal and state governmental machinery in a number of instances to further the antinuclear cause.

At the federal level, the Nuclear Regulatory Commission (NRC) offers a means for nuclear opponents to confront the nuclear industry. Every nuclear plant must receive two licenses from the NRC, a construction license and an operating license. To obtain these licenses, hearings must be held. At these hearings, critics need only raise doubts about a proposed reactor for a full-scale investigation to be carried out by the staff of the commission.

A full-scale investigation will hold up the construction of a nuclear reactor for a period of time. Even when the NRC rejects the arguments of the critics and proceeds to license the plant, the case can be taken to the federal courts. In 1975, nuclear opponents were able to persuade a U.S. court of appeals that the NRC had failed to take into consideration problems involving waste disposal and the reprocessing of fuel.

Antinuclear forces now have articulate spokespersons in the House of Representatives and the Senate. Senator Mike Gravel (D-Alaska) and Congressman Hamilton Fish (R-N.Y.) have introduced a bill known as the Nuclear Energy Reappraisal Act. From beginning to end, the act reveals the influence of nuclear opponents. It seeks to bring a halt to the "further expansion of nuclear fission power" until the Office of Technology Assessment carries out a "comprehensive review of the safety, environmental, and economic consequences" of continued nuclear power development.

The study proposed by the two congressmen would cover all aspects of the nuclear industry from the mining of uranium to the problems of waste disposal. The study would be carried on for five years and during this period no new plants would be licensed. Furthermore, the bill declares that the Office of Technology Assessment must not rely primarily on the expertise and advice of any group that forms a part of the nuclear industry, but should seek testimony from a wide variety of sources, including consumer experts, environmentalists, and scientists and engineers who are independent of pronuclear interests.

Section 5 of the act requires that the final report submitted to Congress include recommendations on "the short-term and long-term genetic effects of low-level radiation" and other health problems. The final report is required to evaluate the economic impact of nuclear expansion—from the costs of uranium fuel to the expenses involved in reprocessing and waste disposal. Finally, the act suggests that before licensing of plants can be renewed after the completion of the study, Congress would have to decide that "nuclear fission plants are clearly superior to other energy sources, including renewable energy sources."

As yet, the Nuclear Energy Reappraisal Act has not passed either house of the Congress. But its existence underlines a new concern among lawmakers that nuclear energy can be dangerous and costly. Another sign that Congress has been influenced by the arguments of the critics is the Plutonium Recovery Control Act of 1975, a bill introduced by Les Aspin (a Democrat from Wisconsin) and other members of the House of Representatives. This bill seeks to control the spread of plutonium by requiring strict licensing laws for plutonium reactors.

Several of the most striking successes of the antinuclear movement have come at the state level. Several states have recently passed new laws or strengthened old ones in order to toughen the regulation of the nuclear industry. In 1975, for instance, both houses of the Vermont legislature required that the legislature approve any future nuclear projects in the state. The legislature was acting in response to demands from consumers and environmentalists and from the Vermont Public Interest Research Group, an antinuclear organization. Complaints from the consumers and environmentalists centered around the high costs of electric bills due to the construction of a nuclear plant by Vermont Yankee, a utility company. Since the passage of the Vermont law, no new reactor has been constructed in the state.

In 1976, the California legislature passed a law similar to the Vermont law that gave the legislature stronger jurisdiction over nuclear power plant construction. The new restraints on the nuclear industry came as a result of demands from antinuclear groups and from the public that more controls needed to be placed on nuclear energy expansion. The legislature required that the state energy commission must now certify that fuel reprocessing and waste disposal programs exist for all future plants before they are constructed. Furthermore, the legislature reserved the right to review and approve the commission's findings before plant construction began.

In several other states, legislators have responded to demands for greater regulation of the nuclear industry by simply giving state regulatory commissions more power. This takes the problem out of the hands of the elected lawmakers and places it in the hands of the professionals who staff the commissions. This has been done in Iowa, Oregon, Florida, and Nebraska.

In Wisconsin, the Public Service Commission asserted on its own that it could review nuclear plant safety considerations, since these considerations involved questions of rate increases and costs to the consumer. This decision was significant because federal law requires that all safety problems are the responsibility of the federal government. By declaring the issue of safety an economic issue, the Wisconsin commission had greatly expanded its own powers over the nuclear industry.

The Connecticut legislature has also been active. In 1975, it set up the Nuclear Power Evaluation Council to look into the question of state regulation of nuclear plants. The council has been given the power to study a broad spectrum of nuclear-related problems including safety and economics. The Connecticut legislature, in the same year, passed a bill forbidding utility companies from advertising on political questions at public expense. Advertisement was deemed political when it tried to sway public opinion on important issues, such as the nuclear energy controversy.

Another path open to the antinuclear movement is the "initiative process." In twenty-two states and many cities, proposed legislation can be taken out of the hands of the legislators and city council members and put to a public vote, if a sufficient number of valid signatures on a petition are acquired over a given period of time. The first nuclear initiative took place in Eugene, Oregon, in 1970. A group of environmentalists, angered by the city's utility company and its plans to build a reactor, demanded that the issue be decided by vote. When the initiative was held, the people of Eugene rejected the new plant.

In 1976, the people in eight states voted on initiatives aimed at restricting the growth of the nuclear industry. In California, Oregon, Washington, Montana, Arizona, Colorado, and Ohio, these initiatives were readily defeated. But in Missouri, where the antinuclear forces concentrated their efforts on the question of increased utility bills due to nuclear plant costs, the initiative won.

The failure in seven states, however, did not dampen the hopes of nuclear opponents. Many believed that the California legislature had passed its laws of 1976 restricting nuclear plants because of the threat of the initiative. Others pointed out that the antinuclear movement was still in its infancy and that the initiative process, even when it ended in defeat, provided a means to bring important questions about nuclear energy before the public. "These campaigns have made the hazards and costs of nuclear power a national issue," declared Bruce Rosenthal of Ralph Nader's Critical Mass. By 1978, Montana and Hawaii had passed initiatives, and in many other states and cities they were under consideration.

Antinuclear activists have used the office of the attorney general and the courts of several states to advance the antinuclear cause. In New Mexico, Kentucky, Vermont, and New Jersey, nuclear opponents have persuaded state attorneys general to challenge plans for nuclear expansion by utility companies. This allows the opponents more time to concentrate on other matters, while the state carries out the costly and time-consuming details involved in litigation against the nuclear industry.

The most highly publicized antinuclear court trial to date involved the case of Karen Silkwood, who worked at a plant of the Kerr-McGee Chemical Corporation in Oklahoma that manufactured fuel rods for reactors. Through her experience in the plant, Ms. Silkwood became deeply concerned about the safety of her fellow workers. She complained to her superiors about carelessness she observed in the handling of plutonium, but was largely ignored. On three successive days in November 1974, she showed up for work contaminated with radiation.

The source of the contamination was plutonium, which was found in her home refrigerator. No one seemed to know just how it got there. Spokespersons for the Kerr-McGee plant claimed that she had stolen it in order to contaminate herself and dramatize the lax conditions she claimed existed at the plant. Nuclear opponents guessed that the plutonium had been planted in her refrigerator. Whatever the source of the plutonium, Karen Silkwood died in a car accident on November 13, 1974, reportedly as she was on her way to a meeting with an atomic worker's union official and a news reporter. She was to have given them evidence of the plant's violations of federal regulations.

Silkwood's family sued Kerr-McGee. The issue at stake

was the safety of the plant, not the nature of her death. On May 18, 1979, after twenty-one hours of deliberation, the jury awarded the family $10.5 million in damages. It was a victory for her relatives, but it was also a victory for the antinuclear activists who had urged the family to sue and used the trial to publicize the hazards of nuclear energy.

If upheld by higher courts, the decision will prove to be one of the strongest indictments of the nuclear industry to date. Not only was an important company found guilty of negligence and irresponsibility, but in the course of the trial, the presiding judge declared that plutonium was so inherently dangerous that Kerr-McGee could be held liable for damages even if negligences were not proved against the company.

Like the civil rights and anti–Vietnam War movements of an earlier time, the antinuclear movement has on occasion resorted to demonstrations and sit-ins. These forms of protest help to dramatize the antinuclear cause and underline the seriousness and dedication of the activists. Demonstrations have been held at the Seabrook reactor in New Hampshire by the Clamshell Alliance. Another was held by Project Survival in Palo Alto, California, to commemorate the death of Karen Silkwood.

One of the largest antinuclear demonstrations so far took place in Washington, D.C., on May 6, 1979. Estimates of the crowd varied from 60,000 to 100,000, but whatever its size, the presence of so many people proved that nuclear energy had become a serious concern to a significant portion of the American population. Prominent antinuclear activists like Governor Jerry Brown of California, actress Jane Fonda, and Ralph Nader spoke to the demonstrators and lent their support to the occasion. For many of those in Washington, the march was only the first of many that would follow.

One note of disagreement was sounded, however, by a longtime nuclear critic. Dr. Arthur Tamplin, whose work has revealed many of the dangers involved in radioactivity, refused to attend the rally although he worked at the Natural

Resources Defence Council in Washington. Dr. Tamplin said that he could not agree with the extremism of some of those who organized the march. "To equate the operators of nuclear power plants with mass murderers," he was quoted as saying, "is more than I could stand." Like all political movements, the antinuclear movement seemed to have reached a stage where moderates and radicals divide and go their separate ways.

It is impossible to say how the nuclear energy controversy will end. Two implacable groups now face one another and neither seems likely to yield. Nor is the attitude of the American public clear and easy to read. Parts of the country appear to be in the antinuclear camp while other sections remain pronuclear. The city of Austin, Texas, for instance, held a nuclear initiative which took place a few days after the accident at Three Mile Island, a time when fears about nuclear energy ran high. The initiative failed and the people of Austin chose to allow their utility company to continue its plans for a new reactor.

In the opinion of this author, the most likely energy future for the United States is a "mixed" energy program. Nuclear research and development will continue, but at a slower rate than previously predicted. At the same time, new discoveries in solar energy and other forms of energy now advocated by the nuclear critics will offer additional sources of energy and power. One hundred years ago, the primary source of power in America was wood. By 1900, it had become coal which was later replaced by oil and natural gas. Only forty years ago, nuclear energy was generally unknown and a thing of the future. Tomorrow or next week the breakthrough may come that will allow us to discard nuclear energy, just as we replaced wood and coal with other forms of energy in the past. There seems to be no reason to conclude that science and technology have achieved all that they can achieve in the field of energy.

FOR FURTHER READING

An asterisk (*) denotes a book of particular interest to a younger reader.

There have been many good books written on the atom and atomic energy, but three of the most helpful are Selig Hecht's *Explaining the Atom* * (New York: Viking, 1954); Heinz Haber's *Our Friend the Atom* * (New York: Dell, 1956); and L. A. Redman's *Nuclear Energy* * (London: Oxford University Press, 1963). On the current energy crisis and its implications, see John Maddox's *Beyond the Energy Crisis* (London: Hutchinson, 1975) and Timothy J. Healy's *Energy and Society* (San Francisco: Boyd & Fraser, 1976).

Among those books that strongly favor nuclear energy are the following: Gordon Dean's *Report on the Atom* * (New York: Knopf, 1953); S. E. Hunt's *Fission, Fusion and the Energy Crisis* * (New York: Pergamon Press, 1974); Glen Seaborg's and William Corliss's *Man and Atom: Shaping a New World Through Nuclear Technology* (New York: Dutton, 1971); and S. D. Freeman's *Energy, The New Era* (New York: Vintage, 1974). Hunt's book is excellent. The reader is also reminded to check the current and back issues of *Science 80,** *Scientific American*, *Science*, and *American Scientist* where numerous articles appear generally in support of nuclear energy.

John J. Berger's *Nuclear Power: The Unviable Option* * (Palo Alto: Ramparts Press, 1976) presents one of the most thorough cases against nuclear energy. Likewise opposed to nuclear power is Barry Commoner, *The Poverty of Power* * (New York: Knopf, 1976) and *The Politics of Energy* * (New York: Knopf, 1979). Commoner also gives interesting arguments in favor of solar energy and other alternative sources of power to satisfy the energy crisis. Peter Faulkner, editor, *The Silent Bomb: A Guide to the Nuclear Energy Controversy* * (New York: Vintage, 1977); Ralph Nader and John Abbotts, *The Menace of Atomic Energy* * (New York: W. W. Norton & Co., 1977); and Dr. Helen Caldicott, *Nuclear Madness* * (Brookline, Massachusetts: Autumn Press, 1978) are among the more staunch opponents of nuclear energy. An important publication by men and women of science opposed to nuclear energy is the Union of Concerned Scientists' *The Nuclear Fuel Cycle: A Survey of the Public Health, Environmental, and National Security Effects of Nuclear Power* (Cambridge: The MIT Press, 1975).

The reader is reminded that many of the books mentioned above have bibliographies of their own that can serve as guides to further reading and research into the pros and cons of nuclear energy.

INDEX

ABOUT THE AUTHOR

Stephen Goode is a former member of the history faculty of Rutgers University. He holds degrees in history from Davidson College, the University of Virginia, and Rutgers.

Mr. Goode is presently engaged in research and writing in Washington, D.C. He has authored a number of books for Franklin Watts, including *Assassination! Kennedy, King, Kennedy; The National Defense System;* and *Eurocommunism.*